GROWING

MAGIC

MUSHROOMS

AT HOME

Self-Guide to Psilocybin Mushrooms Cultivation and Safe Use, Benefits and Side Effects. The Healing Powers of Hallucinogenic and Magic Plant Medicine!

By

Paul Jason Stamets

DISCLAIMER

© Copyright 2021

Introduction

In case you invest a little energy perusing the published writing or the different Sites regarding the matter of Psilocvbe mushroom development, you will rapidly see the dizzying exhibit of methods that one can involve to grow these mushrooms. For a beginner growing mushrooms can be a troublesome illustration to learn. Early disappointments (frequently among the most disastrous) can be so disheartening for certain individuals that they surrender totally. In our case over and over we were prepared to hurl everything and return to doing something simple, similar to brain surgery. However, at that point, we found brain surgery wasn't close to as much fun, got back to growing mushrooms, and in the end our victories were more staggering than our disappointments. We can guarantee you that a similar will turn out as expected for you assuming you stay with it notwithstanding anything mishaps you might experience en route.

We have attempted to present to the reader a bunch of mushroom development methods that are straightforward and dependable enough to essentially minimize the number of issues and disappointments that could emerge. A framework is, if not secure We have looked to stay away from methods that are confusing or present an excessive number of decisions for the cultivator at each phase of the process. Instead, we have attempted to direct the beginner from one finish of the mushroom life cycle to the next in the easiest and most direct course conceivable. The methods we present are among those that we have found the easiest and best in our hands. You should not interpret the oversight of some other methods from this aide as an implied scrutinization of their benefits. Existence keeps us from describing or commenting on every one of the potential ways you could grow these mushrooms. You could almost certainly find achievement using one of these elective methods, and we could never need to prevent you from additional trial and error, assuming that is your longing. This book isn't intended to be the final word about psilocybin-containing mushrooms. Its main intention is just to open the beginner to essential and solid methods for growing a few of them. The thing about beginners is that once they get rolling, they don't remain beginners for a long time, and before long outgrow their initial training. Whenever you have seen firsthand the way that these mushrooms grow, you will normally begin to see different roads for investigation and trial and error. To have outgrown our methods is to have demonstrated their worth as devices for learning. Something else you could see in reading this book is that it contains methods for cultivating mushrooms for a bigger scope, supposed "mass methods. After some pondering, we chose to cover the subject of enormous-scope development for two reasons. The methods we portray here should give any reader a sizable amount of psilocybin to keep one's loved ones "bemushroomed" for quite a long time. On the off chance that you find you have an excess, we urge you to (carefully) offer them as opposed to selling them in the open market. Additionally, while growing or possessing this mushroom in any amount is unlawful in many nations, growing them in mass as well as selling them is simply asking for the inconvenience. The limited-scale methods we portray are undeniably more fit for anybody trying to stay under the radar, and the most effective way to try not to be broken is to keep out of "the business" in any case. Methods for growing mushrooms of each kind (including the Psilocybes) on both little and huge scopes can be viewed in a few of the books in our further reading list. This is the ideal manual for beginners. Experienced growers will likewise see the value in the itemized instructions on working with spores, fluid culture, agar plates, and in any event, making your own spore syringe. Book will cause you to feel like you have a companion guiding you through each basic detail to cause you to feel as good and certain as could really be expected. This guide centers only around development. Reading through the Chapter by chapter guide uncovers the exhaustiveness and level of detail not found somewhere else. It is the ideal book for potential growers prepared to begin today and who would rather not feel stalled with pointless authentic or logical conversations. It additionally explains inaccurate information found in websites composed by non-growers, and includes subtleties others forget about. Dissimilar to different assets, inside the book, the entire process is spread out plainly and linearly for convenience.

Instructions to Peruse This Book

We emphatically recommend you read this book from one cover to another, front to back, each section in turn, in the request introduced. On the off chance that like us you stand out in length, go ahead and skip around and read the book in anything request you like. Simply ensure that by the day's end you have perused the book in its total before you endeavor any of the tests within, even before you begin gathering your equipment and materials, for two significant reasons. Mushroom development, first of all, is a confounded and weird process, and isn't the kind of work for which everybody is essentially appropriate. It is not at all impossible that after reading this book you will find that you don't have the opportunity or fortitude to find success with it. That is fine. Better that you sort that out before you invest any further time and cash in the project. The last thing we believe should do is deter you from trying. We genuinely accept that the methods we present are straightforward enough for pretty much anybody to effectively perform. We simply need to ensure you truly understand what you are in for should you decide to check them out. Second, and maybe more significant, if you require some investment to internalize whatever number of the thoughts and processes we present as could be expected under the circumstances before beginning, you will prevail undeniably more rapidly than you otherwise would. We sorted out this part in the most difficult way possible. It was only after we had perused each book we could find regarding the matter again and again and truly felt like we comprehended what should occur, that things happened how they should. At the end of the day, it was just when we could see with our mind's eye what we should find in this present reality that our analyses finally started to prove to be fruitful. We trust that this book is introduced so that after reading it, you will comprehend what you will do and why, and you will encounter quick achievement.

Chapter 1

Mushrooms in General

The term mushroom implies in everyday a fungus however generally it is the fruiting body of certain parasites which produce and disseminate spores. Like any remaining organisms, they need Chlorophyll and hence can't deliver their food. They develop saprophytically or once in a while harmoniously upon other dead and living plants separately to obtain natural matter as food. Mushrooms are variable in size and shape. Many have caps and tails yet a few assortments are without tails. A few assortments even produce organic product bodies beneath the ground. There is an enormous number of species growing wild, while many are edible, some are profoundly toxic. The assortment of bright and assortment of shapes of mushrooms is by and by since the days of yore. Auricularia, Lentinus exodus, Agaricus bisporus and

Volvariella volvacea were gathered in China and France and somewhere else on the planet. In India, they have begun to develop mushrooms in 1943.

Significance of Mushroom Development

Mushrooms are well known for their delicacy and flavor. They are superb wellsprings of vitamins, proteins, and minerals. They are a great wellspring of Vitamins B, folic corrosive, the blood-building vitamin, valuable in pallid conditions. They likewise contain pantothenic corrosive, vitamin B-12, ascorbic corrosive, and the forerunner of vitamin A and D. They are additionally a great wellspring of phosphorus, potassium, and iron, copper, contain all fundamental amino acids especially L-lysine and L-tryptophan. Mushrooms contain the least amount of sugars along with fats, subsequently an entirely significant eating routine for those suffering from diabetes and heart issues. They additionally contain compounds fit for preventing respiratory failure, diabetes, and disease, infections because of microbes, parasites, infections, and protozoa. Edible mushrooms have been suggested by the FAO as food, contributing to the protein nourishment of developing nations relies generally upon grains. Mushrooms help treat numerous human afflictions.

With the increasing populace, and food request issues in developing and immature nations, mushrooms can assume a significant part to improve human eating routines, especially in India where an enormous segment of the populace are veggie lovers. It is an ideal method for recycling agro-squanders which are accessible plentifully. The spent fertilizer from mushroom ranches is a decent natural excrement and a superior substrate for biogas creation. It is a work-intensive indoor activity that, helps the landless, little, and marginal ranchers to raise their income, and different financial activities can make gainful business, particularly for the jobless/underemployed youth, more vulnerable segments of the general public, and ladies. Our nation has assets, and the potential for huge scope creation of mushrooms both for homegrown utilization and commodity. These are developed everywhere. However, mushroom development is known from the days of yore its development in India began in 1943 when Volvariella voilvacea was developed at Coimbatore, and Agaricus bisporus and Pleurotus solar caju were developed in 1966 and 1970 separately. Despite it, mushroom development in India is just 0.09% of world creation. Be that as it may, the Indian Govt. has perceived the significance of mushrooms under changed conditions and established a public examination place at Solan, Himachal Pradesh where an intensive exploration has been done on various parts of mushrooms, their development to inspire individuals of India for the utilization of mushroom as a piece of their eating regimen.

Characterization of Edible Mushrooms

Edible mushrooms are arranged according to ordered position as well as their normal environment. The scientific classification of mushrooms is a fascinating field, both morphological characteristics of the natural product body, spore creation, and spore tone ended up being valuable. The spore print which can be obtained by placing the cut natural product body on white paper is covered with a bell jar for the short term.

Chapter 2

Specifics of Psilocybin, Or "Magic," Mushrooms

In practically all cases, indeed, Psilocybin is leaned to the timetable I of the Controlled Substances Act, which makes it against the law to develop Psilocybin, and that implies producing such mushrooms for individual use or spreading. Be that as it may, they might be used for specialized research and are controlled conditions with a selective permit from the Medication Requirement Administration. At any rate, in many cases, mushrooms containing Psilocybin itself are unlawful in the government and different states, and this kind of mushroom development, ownership, and deal is the reason for the capture. A crucial ingredient found in numerous psychoactive mushrooms is Psilocybin. However, Psilocybin is taken as a successful medicinal portion (around 3-4 mg) that is a standard portion of medicine ranging from 14mg - 30 mg. This kind of portion is effectively rehearsed in clinics. The impacts of Psilocybin on the brain are portrayed by its dynamic ingredient Psilocin. It is generally tracked down in the wild or home-reaped mushrooms and is taken orally in the type of eating dried covers and stems or saturated with high temp water or the type of tea, and its most widely recognized portion taken is ranging from 1 to 2.5 grams. It is sold in dried or fresh mushroom structures, and the most well-known or renowned specie is PSILOCYBE cubensis.

History of Psilocybin Mushrooms

Psilocybin mushrooms have been created for millennia among locals and individuals all over the planet that includes including in Europe and America. It was made popular again in 1957 through a paper that highlighted an American broker and mushroom enthusiast R. Gordon Wasson, and it was published in Life Magazine. Later on, following 4 years he ran over an indigenous clan who were using psychoactive mushrooms in Mexico, and after returning he brought some of it. He gave it to a Swiss scientist named Albert Hofmann, who disconnected Psilocybin to foster a combination at Sandoz Drugs that later on for research purposes began producing 2mg tablets. For the following twenty years or something like that, a large number of dosages of Psilocybin were overseen in clinical preliminaries. Specialists, researchers, and proficient mental healthcare who believed psilocybin to be anticipated medicine for the treatment of an expansive scope of specialist analysis that included liquor addiction, schizophrenia, chemical imbalance disorder, fanatical impulsive condition, depression, and nervousness. For different strict practices, profound works on, exploring mental and emotional, and improving mental and emotional prosperity, many individuals were given psilocybin mushrooms and other hallucinogenics. Even though it had a long history and was a piece of exploration among experts yet was later on in 1970, Psilocybin and

Psilocin were leaned to Timetable I of the controlled substances Act. This class is portrayed to have "profoundly conceivable oppressive" that is vigorously criminalized classification for drugs that likewise subtleties for "No clinical use," however while considering Psilocybin, which gives extremely essential realities in actuality for both depicted previously.

The effects of Psilocybin Mushroom

The utilization and its subtleties are depicted above, yet the impermanent aftereffects of hallucinogenic medications like Psilocybin Mushroom shift massively and arranging it is muddled. Their belongings and results are different for different individuals at better places, and at various times, that is an incredible factor. In any case, its consequences for cognizance and discernment are notable, and its belongings Psilocybin impacts stay around 4 to 6 hours with a peak of 2 to 3 hours in the wake of consuming it. These impacts are very much depicted, which include an increase in the faculties. For instance, the time-changing impact that better portrays as minutes feel like hours, imaginary items, or genuine articles would want to move, a few shapes, and emerging examples of either having eyes shut or open. It likewise brings not common discussions, personality insight, and an excited state of mind. The response of the individual is impacted by the individual convictions, mindsets, and mental state, likewise the conditions, individuals around him, and the surroundings he is living in. These varieties come in light of the distinction of individuals from others, the variety of encounters those results immensely unique. It very well may be connected with unfriendly encounters or significant, meaningful, and hopeful encounters.

Psilocybin Mushroom as Medicine

Confirmations show yes. It was viewed as a completely lawful, financially-subsidized research program during the twentieth century that painstakingly examined numerous mental sicknesses, individual and otherworldly turn of events, and imagination, which were gainful. Notwithstanding, after the banning of Psilocybin in 1970, clinical examination to evaluate clinical well-being and exploration for medicinal designs was halted. The examination ended when it was limited until the last part of the 1990s and the beginning of 2000. Today, many examination papers, studies, and books are being composed to assess the medicinal security and helpfulness of such hallucinogenics that additionally include psilocybin. The examination before banning doesn't agree with the principles of ongoing times. Yet, the scientists and their promising findings superseding the past examination findings have uncovered the resurgence of the modern and most thorough exploration potential, on the advantages of such hallucinogenics to treat nervousness, depression, migraine, liquor addiction, drug harmful all, and fanatical habitual condition to additional studying its consequences for the brain psychotics. Since the examination process and its consent are especially costly, a large portion of the exploration is financed by the not-for-profit association. Because of its listing in Timetable, I drug the scholar and governmental institutions don't support it.

Significant Healthy Impacts of Psilocybin Mushrooms

For the most part, mental dangers are credited to the utilization of hallucinogenic medications, and the actual impacts are intriguing. The most un-poisonous medication makes actual impacts. Be that as it may, through different analyses of a few creatures, dangerous portions are determined. There are uncommon cases of people that are found dead by the typical portions of Psilocybin Mushroom, and actual impacts shift from one individual to another. Enlarged students increased pulse, raised circulatory strain that is for the most part gentle, and are the steady responses of using such medications, although it is taken as emotionally intensifying incidental effects. Yet, mental impacts like a feeling of vomiting, numbing, quakes, and increased sweat are accounted for impacts that likewise include nervousness, depression, and feeling fits of anxiety. There were uncommon actual consequences for people for a drawn-out premise. That was tracked down straightforwardly described by the pharmacology of psilocybin.

Risks of Psilocybin Mushrooms

Cases of death are uncommon in the utilization of psilocybin, and the poisonousness levels are lacking. Current epidemiological investigations have shown lower mental disorders and self-destruction rates for those individuals who have utilized hallucinogenics like psilocybin. The risks from psilocybin are reliant upon its utilization and use limit and are especially not the same as liquor abuse, narcotics, and sedatives those outcomes in predictable physical and mental impacts. The negative defying contentions can be decreased by mindfulness and training of psilocybin impacts yet needs specific regard for all matters and information. It isn't viewed as additive or can cause over-the-top utilization of it. The physical and mental difficulties due to intensive encounters can make people limit the utilization and recurrence of the purpose of psilocybin. Besides, the human body makes a tolerance against psilocybin. Subsequently, individuals using psilocybin need to increase the portion of rehashed use, or they need a lot higher portion of rehashed use, which makes it especially hard to influence, after over and over using for over four days. Since human brain receptors are involved the impacts are comparable. The cross-tolerance arises with LSD and psilocybin that implies the absorbing or psilocybin decreases assuming LSD is required one day. Indeed, it is unlawful given being recorded, in plan I of the controlled substances Act which makes it against the law to have its ownership, development of psilocybin-producing mushrooms for individual use, or its dispersion. Be that as it may, the logical examination under a firmly controlled climate and conditions in the wake of obtaining extraordinary confirmation from the medication requirement administration can be utilized. However, individuals who were captured for criminal belonging, development, or dissemination were guaranteed innocence because government regulation doesn't have a rundown of types of psilocybin mushrooms. In many cases, psilocybin-containing mushrooms are unlawful according to government regulation, governmentally and statewide.

Chapter 3

Prominent Psilocybin Species

There are approximately 30,000 reported types of mushroom growing growths all over the planet. Of these, around 100 kinds of assortments contain Psilocybin or related synthesis. A large portion of them are found in Genera Psilocybin and Panaeolus, and some are found somewhere else in Inocybe, Conocybe, and Gymnopilus-land. Few out of every odd one of these varieties contains Psilocybin and, surprisingly, those that can distinguish it.

We present the ongoing techniques for cultivating two sorts of Psilocybin mushrooms:

Compost inhibiting technique for species like Psilocybe cubensis (the complex of the interrelated lignicolous strategy.) Wood-inhabiting species, for example, Psilocybe azurescens and P.cyanescens.

We chose to zero in on these specific species for a few significant reasons: they produce moderately high measures of psilocybin, have a long history of development, and develop the natural product in dependable and generally high amounts and agreeable circumstances. Furthermore, they offer indoor development prospects. Albeit other famous assortments take special care of these standards, the two assortments we have picked should deliver a lot of Psilocybin for any tenacious individual.

The explanation is to get to know these species, including their regular environment and behavior so you can comprehend their fundamental science as you begin to work with them. This book isn't a "field guide" and isn't to do your inquiry and gather these species from nature. Foraging for mushrooms, whether for food or Psilocybin, needs a lot of information and expertise. Poisoning because of misidentification is a genuine and possibly destructive danger. Assuming you are interested in collecting your mushrooms, we suggest that you have a decent glance at the most extreme and a few helpful field guides. Tell you to Counsel straightforwardly with specialists who know your fungus. Odds are good that you have a neighborhood mycological society or club where there are individuals who train you what you want to figure out how to distinguish wild mushrooms.

Psilocybe cubensis is one of the most generally developed psychoactive mushrooms for both verifiable and organic reasons. Universally, it is one of the main normal specie for psilocybin viewed in the wild and is, in this way, the most broadly utilized and generally consumed well-known. Generally, it is at most extreme cases Psilocybe cubensis fruiting that emerges from a plate of cased wheat berries.

It is likewise the most straightforward to develop, as it proves to be fruitful on many substrates, and in various environmental circumstances. Albeit in the wild it develops at last on waste, under development it develops natural products on any substrates on a significant degree of carbon and nitrogen: from cereal straw, grain, grass, straw, wood, paper, or cardboard, whenever added with protein. Most mushroom assortments are different in their turn of events and organic product necessities, but not in the P. Cubensis. Combined with its significant intensity, makes it is one of the most incredible species for a beginner-level cultivator to develop. We start with Psilocybe cubensis because it is the simplest to develop. The kind of mushrooms contains psilocybin. Individuals are generally acquainted with it and while combining the creation of its quickly developing profoundly rhizomorphic mycelia.

It is a bountiful early stage. It has an enormous, intense organic product, and productive spore creation that is combined to make the most models of Basidiomycetes. Whenever you have worked with P. Cubensis for some time and come out as comfortable with the mushroom life cycle, you are prepared to work with assortments of mushrooms that act in additional unpretentious ways. P. cubensis is a warm tropical mushroom that develops plentifully on fertilizer or excrement of cows, ponies, and elephants or soils that are blended in with their compost. It tends to be established in any place on the planet with damp, warm environments, including Southeast Asia, Australia, India, Mexico, Focal America, North-South America, and the Caribbean. In the US, it is tracked down for the most part in the southeastern US in the pre-summer or late spring, from Florida to the Texas coast.

It is one of the biggest animal categories with psilocybin, with 0.5 to 5 inches across, and 8-inch-long thick stems. At the point when developed on grain or rice, they are generally little in size, however on fertilizer or compost, they can deliver tremendous, strong natural products. It produces dull purple-earthy colored spore prints.

At the point when taken care of, the psilocybin cubensis swelled and develops a blue surface. Albeit the blue response frequently indicates the presence of psilocybin in mushrooms, such proof itself can't be viewed as convincing proof, as other irrelevant contagious mixtures behave something very similar. Additionally, the shortfall of a blue response doesn't be guaranteed to preclude the presence of particles, for example, psilocybin-like particles in mushrooms.

The bluing response happens when psilocin is oxidized into not portray dull blue synthetic. Mushrooms have a lower level of psilocin, yet a perceptible degree of psilocybin, regardless of their activity, does not become blue.

The P. Cubensis is viewed as normally strong than other dynamic species. It can contain up to 1.2% of psilocybin, psilocin, and baeocystin, a normal of 0.5%, or 0.5 mg/gram. Albeit, such a normal is a valuable standard for comparing the intensity of one specie with another specie. It is essential to take note that this intensity may likewise change generally among mushrooms of similar species.

Certain strains, or similar strains developed under various substrates or various circumstances, can show extraordinary changes in power. Albeit a similar culture can shift starting with one flush and then onto the next, the second and third flush is normally the most powerful.

Wood-loving Psilocybes, even though Psilocybe cubensis are not difficult to develop, there is a kind of home development that is ineffectively shaped: outside. In the woodland, it develops outside and might be required in the nursery or the wild, however, there is no genuine advantage in doing so.

The two main benefits of establishing an outside mushroom garden are that they can be both perpetual and clandestine. You set it up on the edges, target it until it proves to be fruitful, develop the mushrooms, and in the wake of receiving it afterward forget about it until the process rehashes the same thing one year from now. When established, a mystery mushroom fix should be pretty much self-adequate and fretful, except for natural products.

For different reasons, Psilocybe cubensis doesn't meet this kind of arrangement. To start with, its natural products quickly and over and over until its substrates get a lack in supplements are additionally drained, and more often than not, it isn't viewed as perpetual. Second, it becomes on and bears various natural products on different substrates, however in this way has an entire host of other undesirable organic entities. However long the fruiting substrate is kept clean, the mushrooms are colonized by molds and microbes before they are fully grown.

In this manner, it is constantly filled indoors in a painstakingly controlled condition. All things considered, being a warm exotic animal variety, it doesn't fill well in a chilly climate and certainly doesn't endure the underneath freezing temperatures in many spots during the winter months. Luckily for the new mushroom landscaper, there are bunches of psilocybe that are perfectly working.

It is the lignicolous or wood-loving specie that has a gathering of related psilocybin-containing mushrooms. They develop on wood chips or bark mulch, and they are classified as "caramel-covered" psilocybin to owe to their appearance. This gathering includes around 10 species, including psilocybin cyanescens, P zaurescens, and P Cyanofibrillosa, local to the Pacific Northwest of the US, Eastern European types of P. serbica and P. sllbaerugil and P. tasmaniana, which are from Australia and New Zealand.

Psilocybe Cyanofibrillosa Specie

Psilocybe cyanofibrillosa is a little wood-loving psilocybe that is normal along the Pacific shoreline of the US, from San Francisco to British Columbia. It isn't thought of as especially intense, containing just 0.25% alkaloids by dry weight. In any case, there is evidence to recommend that a higher extent of the alkaloids in this species can be drained on drying than in others, making fresh Psilocybe cyanofibrillosa examples surprisingly powerful.

Psilocybe Bohemica Specie

Psilocybe bohemica is the relative of focal Northern Europe, likewise belonging to the North American lignicolous Psilocybe species tracked down in Germany, Austria, and the Czech Republic. It looks like Psilocybe azurescens and P. cyanofibrillosa and is somewhat less strong than Psilocybe cyanescens averaging around with regards to dry weight. 1.1% alkaloids.

Psilocybe Subaeruginosa Specie

Psilocybe subaeruginosa is a relative of Psilocybe azurescens, from Australia and Tasmania. It seems to be Psilocybe azurescens, however marginally shorter in height, and is practically identical to Psilocybe cyanescens.

Compound investigations of this species are restricted.

Psilocybe Cyanescens Specie

Psilocybe cyanescens is moderately powerful, normally tracked down in Canada from the Pacific Northwest to San Francisco. Its most distinctive element is the undulating cap margin, which has nicknamed it is mushroom "wavy covers." It develops on wood chips or wood trash on the yards, garden beds, and country roads along mulched ways. At the point when youthful, its mushrooms have a prominent, coordinate ("web-like") fractional cover, which isolates quickly when ready. Psilocybe cyanescens has a generally high Psilocin content and is wounded when transforms into blue rapidly.

Psilocybe azurescens Specie

The most intense known is the Psilocybe azurescens mushroom. The presence of Psilocybe azurescens is like Psilocybe azurescens, then again, actually the resulting seems to be the last species, and frequently shows like an areola knock on the focal point of its cap. The backwoods generally develops on wood trash in sandy waterfront soils, frequently living under grasses. Psilocybe azurescens, specifically, has a high baeocystin content, which could be represented by a supposedly novel hallucinogenic "signature." Clients by and large report that it delivers a significant and profound dependable impact, without critical actual inconvenience related to it.

Chapter 4

Hallucinogenic Impacts of Psilocybin Mushrooms

Pharmacology of Psilocybin Mushrooms

Psilocybin is a functioning hallucinogenic piece of hallucinogenic mushrooms. The starting portion to encounter the impacts of dried mushrooms is normally in the scope of 0.2-0.5 grams, even though it relies from one individual to another and shifts distinctively yet a great deal. A medium portion in the scope of 1-2.5 grams, taken orally, typically emanates this impact, which goes on for three to six hours. The intensity contrast is additionally there that defines Psilocybin, and it is multiple times less compelling than LSD and multiple times less powerful than mescaline.

At the point when you take Psilocybin, your body consumes it. Then, at that point, use, and places the substance into psilocin, and it brings about hallucinogenic excitement. Psilocybin and psilocin interact basically with serotonin receptors in the brain and make especially high sympathy for 5-H (serotonin) 2A subtype receptors. In mice, Psilocybin has shown areas of strength with receptors in the center point region of the brain that coordinate tactile encounters. It might explain the impacts of combination, like the experience of combining tactile organs, like hearing tones or tasting sounds - and changing the sensation during a mushroom excursion or outing.

Taking Normal Dosages

The following impacts are not to be inclusive, particularly in a low portion range. They might be dependent on future developments since additional solid, generally addressed information is accessible. This dose limit is for Psilocybe cubensis mushrooms. They can likewise be applied to different varieties that include psilocybin, however, some are more strong by and large.

Miniature Portions (0.05-0.25 G)

The miniature portions are speculative that many individuals include in their week-after-week routine. The thought is to increase the degree of imagination, energy, and consideration and diminish the degree of stress, tension, and emotional instability. A few normal impacts include:

☐ Help mind-sets

☐ Less pressure

☐ Solidness in feelings

☐ Harmony, presence, and mindfulness

☐ Open and self-forgiving

☐ Familiar with Discussion

☐ Depression or uneasiness easing ADD/ADHD, and PTSD

☐ Support, (for example, making positive way of life changes)

☐ stream condition Increasing

☐ Intelligible thinking

☐ Memory Improvement

☐ Imagination Increasing

☐ Reflective state

☐ Unreasonable athletic patience

☐ Increased by and large energy (no stresses over nervousness or resulting crash state)

☐ Mindset Upgrade (positive or negative temperament)

☐ Plausible status of overexcited

☐ Perhaps increasing neuroticism

Mini Portion (0.25-0.75 G)

While a legitimate miniature portion should not be squandered, a little portion of Psilocybin can take you outside your ability to understand - yet it's anything but a completely flight-filled all-out venture. As one individual from our local area establishment, a mini-diet gives you a "full expansion of life, a full progression of feeling" without losing contact with individuals around you. A few normal impacts include:

☐ State of mind swings, gentle upgrade or fervor or temperament improvements

☐ Harmony, presence, and mindfulness

☐ Open and self-forgiving

☐ Intuitive insight

☐ Depression or tension mitigation ADD/ADHD, and PTSD

☐ Consolation, (for example, making positive way of life changes)

☐ stream condition Increasing

☐ Cognizant thinking

☐ Memory Improvement

☐ Faculties are improved

☐ The peaceful act of contemplation

☐ Enjoying actual work and everyday exercises

☐ Increased aversion to light

☐ Exceptionally light methodology, gentle dreams

☐ Possibly hyper status

☐ Trouble paying consideration or breaking thought conditions

☐ The trouble with a few mental works

☐ Uneasiness, incitement or fretfulness, or agitating condition

☐ Trouble or not being agreeable to socializing

Museum Portion (0.5-1.5 Grams)

The impacts of Psilocybin are more known with a gallery portion than with a mini portion, yet an exhibition hall portion doesn't give you a total hallucinogenic encounter. Organic chemist and Pharmacologist Dr. Alexander Shulgin gave this name "Gallery," which alludes to the truth that on this dose, you can in any case partake in open leisure activities (like seeing paintings in an exhibition hall), without getting any prominent consideration. A few normal impacts include:

☐ Increase temperament, happiness, or fervor

☐ Gentle to moderate points of view, (for example, "breathing" conditions)

☐ Compassion increasing

☐ Correspondence stream

☐ Self-examination

☐ Increased stream condition

☐ Sense enhancing

☐ A growing appreciation for music and workmanship

☐ Being imaginative

☐ Mind-set expansion, positive or negative, or temperament amplifying

☐ Changed voice or impression of sound

☐ Time shrinks or elapses rapidly (time elapses all the more leisurely or quicker)

☐ Increased aversion to light

☐ Widening of students

☐ Trouble paying consideration or breaking thought conditions

☐ Trouble cognizance or trouble socializing

☐ Food Disappointment

Moderate Portion (2-3.5 G)

It is where the entire hallucinogenic experience begins. You might see visual deceptions and hallucinations, including designs and investigation, and contortions, like the impression of time and its profundity discernment, are confused. However, with this portion, you can in any case figure out your surroundings - that is all the obvious change. A few normal impacts include:

☐ Groundbreaking point of view

☐ Philosophical insight

☐ The progression of thoughts increased

☐ The growing appreciation for music and expressions

☐ Otherwise, find common things unusual or interesting

☐ Interesting

☐ Going high, then, at that point, arriving at the pinnacle and going low

☐ Positive or negative feelings increasing

☐ Open and shut-eye designs

☐ Blend

☐ Aversion to light

☐ Yawning

☐ Transient and bewilderment

☐ Dread and nervousness feelings ("terrible travel" encounters)

☐ Trouble in intellectual working

☐ Dizziness

☐ Queasiness

Uber Portion (5+ g)

A uber portion is a finished loss of association with the real world. From here, you experience serious deviations, intense hallucinations as well as self-image demise, enchanted encounters, and profound self-information. A few normal impacts include:

☐ Wondrous encounters, enchanted insight

☐ Groundbreaking viewpoint, self-certainty, or philosophical insight

☐ Demise of pride

☐ Exceptionally solid open and shut eyes (life recollections)

☐ Combination

☐ Wasting time or meaning of time does away

☐ Transient and confusion

☐ Compromised engine capabilities

☐ Extreme Trepidation and Uneasiness (Encounters Fluctuate "Terrible Seizures")

☐ Extremely challenging to be an intellect

☐ Dizziness

☐ Sickness

Potential Advantages

Numerous authentic societies have utilized them. Hallucinogenic has a long, established, and grounded standing as a healing and changing specialist. Past insight, the advantages of these strong little treats are generally perceived today. Broad and adaptable utilization of mental mushrooms the parasites are concentrated all through the US and abroad, and there is solid proof that they are indeed energizers for self-awareness. That's what a new report expressed "a single portion of psilocybin creates a critical and lasting decrease in the discouraged state of mind and tension with an increase in personal satisfaction."

Additionally, the otherworldly and significant encounters happened when psilocybin went into the body. Specifically, clinical preliminaries involving lethal malignant growth patients are as of now being directed in the US and abroad. These preliminaries are an endeavor to comprehend the effectiveness of high-portion psilocybin tests directed in a restorative climate to decrease the pressure and nervousness that frequently go with a lethal finding. The outcomes so far have been promising. Under twofold blind, fake treatment-controlled conditions, a high portion of psilocybin has been shown to lessen the indications of mental distress in individuals with a terminal determination, and the impacts of this examination have been critical and lasting.

Furthermore, the growing collection of exploration shows why psilocybin is so valuable since it influences brain adaptability, or, all the more significantly, the brain's capacity to learn, develop, and, above all, its capacity to change.

Expected Risks

Psilocybin is estimated as one of the got psychoactive issues you can get. Truth be told, the 2017 Worldwide Medication Study established that psilocybin is the most secure of all relaxation drugs available. In 2016, just 0.2% of individuals required crisis clinical consideration in the wake of taking psilocybin. That is multiple times not as much as MDMA, LSD, and cocaine. Psilocybin is likewise non-additiveand contains no deadly dosages. It implies that regardless of whether your outing or excursion is awful, you are probably not going to take a lot of psilocybin.

No medicine is supposed to be protected. During beginning and travel, psilocybin can cause a few actual incidental effects like sickness, sweating, deadness, and oxygen hardship. It can likewise cause uneasiness, fits of anxiety, and emotional episodes. A review published in Substance Use and Misuse saw that 33% of those studied experienced tension and distress sooner or later during their outing. Long-haul physical and mental impacts are uncommon. At the point when that occurs, research shows that the reason was simply mental disorders, not mushrooms themselves.

Chapter 5

Equipment Required for Psilocybin Culture

Mushroom development needs equipment, including many specific instruments and things. A portion of these things are extraordinary to such an extent that they must be bought from mushroom growing stores, however, they can be effectively obtained from most nearby sources. A large number of the things you want for a fire are likewise sold for other, more mundane purposes. While making shopping more agreeable, it has the additional advantage of providing better inclusion for the people who need to keep their farming exercises in a position of safety. Tool shops, kitchens and eateries, supply houses, pet stores, home brewing providers, and nursery focuses are the mushroom grower's fortune.

It is a far-reaching rundown of things you can use en route. You want a portion of these before you start. It is another justification for why we suggest that you might peruse the book completely first, conclude how much solace you feel, plan your trials, and shop again. There is no mental understanding of buying 400 pounds of sawdust just to sit in your carport or new lab.

Pressure cooker

It is quite possibly the most involved thing in your cultivating devices shed, so getting a reasonable one from the outset is vital. Since you use it to disinfect or clean moderately huge articles and in amounts, along these lines size is fundamental. From the outset, on the off chance that you can bear the cost of an enormous unit initially required, then, at that point, simply get it because, in the following stages, you should update it. The way to decide what size you should get is the number of quart containers you can securely disinfect at a time. Because of the sporadic shape of the container, they can fit easily even inside a generally enormous strain cooker, to set up a cutoff to process and restrict the number of ingredients you might process at a time.

In this way, we reconnect to get a unit that can keep at least seven-quart containers all at once. There are a lot of choices in the case of strain cooker brand wise and kind wise to get, however, one emerges from the winner as the brand, and that is all American brands produced by Wisconsin Aluminum Foundry. These tension cookers are all around made, profoundly solid, and safe. The enterprise has been in the exchange for a considerable length of time. Also, the plan of their strain cookers has been praised since they were first introduced.

They are made completely of weighty measure cast aluminum and don't have elastic seals or different parts that can be worn. New parts are promptly accessible, and, surprisingly, a 20-year-old unit can be bought at a store or on eBay to make it work. Not likely little, minimal-expense kitchen pressure cookers, which have no chance of precisely measuring internal strain, all Americans have a wide, exceptionally exact dial check. They are additionally intended to keep hold of the vacuum on getting cold, which is fundamental to forestall the starting of sterilizing air in your culture.

There are two normal sorts of strain cookers to browse: those that have steam releasing valve, and those that have a metal-weighted "rocker" at whatever point the tension arrives at over a certain level, it vents out the steam. The last one definite here should be stayed away from, if conceivable, as this quick arrival of tension can heat the fluid inside the cooker, ruin your media, and cause an extensive wreck. Rocker-styled pressure cookers are better usable, however, they should be painstakingly regulated during use to keep away from mishaps. All Americans make two kinds of strain cookers. The stopcock type is what they refer to strain as "disinfectants or sterile," while the weighted rocker is viewed as a tension canner.

Anything brand and model of cooker you pick, ensure it is ready to go, and that you comprehend its activity and security includes well overall, and it better is to peruse the manual. Ensure all seals and gaskets are in phenomenal condition, and the top can be locked from the base. At the point when the tension cooker is compressed, no steam should get away from the seals. If there is, switch off the intensity source, license the cooker to cool totally, and afterward set again the seal. Running a Vaseline dab around the inner edge of the metal-on-metal sort cooker guarantees a tight fit and assists to keep the top fixed to the base during use.

Make certain to add sufficient water to the lower part of the cooker before each time used to allow it to arrive at a profundity of no less than 1/2 inch. Never put equipment on the lower part of the strain cooker straightforwardly and don't allow it to contact the outside walls, where the temperature is most elevated. A significant number of strain cookers accompany a rack or stand plan that is made to hold their items over the outer layer of the water, and all huge American models have crate-shaped lines so the things connect with the cooker. Initially, keep the tension cooker at an increasingly slow temperature, because extremely quick or lopsided heating frameworks can cause it to detonate.

It can take some time, particularly using huge tension cookers. You should see an uninterrupted progression of steam before closing the valve. Leaving the tension cooker unattended isn't the choice, so never leave it unattended. The temperature and strain inside the cooker can vacillate, particularly during the initial heating stages, before the cooker completely balances. To stay away from the cooker blast and to guarantee total sterilization, the cooker should be feeling the squeeze for the whole cycle. Check like clockwork whether it is warmed or overheated by checking its temperature, and change the heating measure depending on the situation. Allow the cooker to chill off leisurely and all alone. At the point when cooker pressure has arrived at its levels, never contact the beyond the cooker and don't utilize cold water to cool it. It can incite the cooker and delivery its items viciously or burst open essentially. At least it delivers a lot of perilous steam. While opening the strain cooker to keep not cleaned air from going in, wrap up a paper towel absorbed liquor around the valve before releasing any tension or venting out. Pressure cookers are possibly perilous. They can have a high temperature, and steam and mishandling can cause serious injuries. Like the noteworthy blade, a tension cooker is a gadget that requests regard and care, and subsequently, offers brilliant advantages.

Petri dish

Petri dishes are low profundity in plastic or glass and are straightforward. They arrive in a variety of shapes, yet the most helpful size for parasitic cultures is 100 x 15 mm. Reusable glass or plastic dishes are dependable and can be autoclaved.

Pre-disinfected dispensable polystyrene dishes come in 20 or 25 sleeves. They're modest, yet they're intended to be utilized just a single time, and they are not required after being utilized. They are not environmentally amicable. The two sorts of Petri dishes can be cleaned using hydrogen peroxide and microwaves.

1. Wash the plates completely with dishwashing cleanser taking unique consideration to annihilating the remaining agar.

2. Put a limited quantity of 3% peroxide in each Petri dish and pivot it around the plate to open it to the whole inner surface. Rehash and cover it.

3. Place every one of the dishes in the microwave and apply medium temperature, until all the peroxide in the plates vanishes.

4. Use the Petri dishes immediately, or keep them in a perfect plastic pack until required.

This procedure is most proficient when combined with the utilization of peroxide in cultures of agar. If working with lacking peroxide agar, it is now protected to utilize pre-clean plastic or autoclaved glass Petri dishes. It is prescribed to add hydrogen peroxide to your cultures to lessen contamination and license you to work with agar in a well-disposed climate. In any case, peroxide can't be utilized in unambiguous situations, for example, the spore germinating process. In these cases, we have found that 50 mm breadth plates are more open to disinfection, in case of their surface decrease. On the off chance that Petri dishes are not accessible, you can utilize a 4-ounce jam container or comparative intensity-resistant glass containers. They have the advantage of being reusable, however, they are not straightforward and occupy two times the room as culture plates.

Media Containers

The media container is portrayed to hold up the fluid media during the sterilization process and dripping Petri plates. Any glass container or jug that can be autoclaved works in such a process, even though you could require a limited neck bottle for dripping. Squeezed apple containers or sparkling water bottles are best for this reason.

Bricklayer Containers: We for the most part utilize standard adjusted ball-type canned containers in quart size. They are promptly accessible, strong, and can be reused for limitless times except if it gets broken. Limited mouth (70 mm) quart containers are great for grain spawning. If you have any desire to attempt the "PF" method, you want a squared container. Before using the artisan containers, check them completely because occasionally get broken or broken, and state of breaks, inspect them to disinfect the breaks from undesirable species that can ruin the process of mushrooming. Try not to shake excessively hard or beat the artisan containers to isolate the grains, because of breaks you could wound yourself. Simply surrender it a light shake and down; you should simply isolate the grains on the off chance that they are firmly bound just to relax them.

Continuously let your tension cooker heat up leisurely. High temperatures can make the broke containers detonate because of the distinction in temperature between their inner side and external side.

Bricklayer container Covers

For culture work, we utilize a piece of plastic cover that is heat safe and effectively modifiable which permits secure gas trade. The ball makes a plastic "stockpiling cap." Albeit they are not great for processing but rather can be autoclaved.

To supplant these edges, you should cautiously bore or drill an opening in the focal point of each cap. At the point when the channel plate is inserted (see next passage), these modified covers permit gases (yet not contaminants) to enter and leave the vial, allowing your culture to openly relax.

Channel Circles

The channel circles are put between the jug cap and the mouth of the container, and the channel plates can make the trading of gas without contamination. They are made of a manufactured fiber that opposes warming and can be disinfected again and again. They are a few millimeters thick and intended to fit in between the mouth and the cap of the container. They change their variety at times when they are presented to substrate or shape spores. Simply douse them short-term in a sanitizer arrangement in 1/fourth piece of it.

An inexpensive substitute is Tyvek, which can be sliced to fit over the cover. Tyvek is manufactured and has different purposes. Rolls can be bought from the building supply store, and are accessible for nothing in little amounts from FedEx or the US Mailing station in the type of enormous mailing envelopes.

Since the Tyvek is thinner and more adaptable than business channel plates, it should be cut into enormous circles more extensive than the mouth of the container and draped somewhere around one inch from the edge of the container. The child is likewise reusable yet should be disposed of after three or four purposes.

Yield Sack

Otherwise called channel fix sacks, these are clear, heat-safe, breezy adaptable plastic packs that are utilized for a huge volume of products to hold. They can be sanitized and have a little square channel on one side for gas trade. They can thickly stack substrate, can be sanitized and inoculated, and afterward fixed by heat sealer. They are great for increasing a lot of products since they are adaptable so the substance of the containers can be controlled or examined for contamination. They lose their versatility when warmed and are generally just appropriate for one use, yet looking great, the sack can be entirely cleaned and disinfected again.

We've seen cultivators use supermarket "broiler packs." Even though they can be autoclaved and intended to work, they need channel patches, give less gas trade, and are a lot thinner for heat sealing. One method for providing such a pack with a touch of breath is to wrap its neck firmly around a thick layer of poly-fill or cotton and seal it firmly with a weighty elastic band. Stove packs can't be moved effectively, as this can increase the tension. Notwithstanding tenderly deal with the product with hands from the external side of the pack.

Surgical and Additional Tools

Sealer

Sealers are utilized to seal and bring forth sacks. Make a point to get sufficiently wide to seal the entire sack, something like 12 inches more extensive across.

The Liquor Light

It is a glass light with a cotton light wick and a metal collar. Loaded up with liquor, it gives an unadulterated fire to sterilize surgical blades and inoculation circles while working.

The Mini-Light

These mini-lights are valuable for sterilizing devices. A decent quality mini-light might have a strong base to keep it upstanding while it sits on the seat top.

The Equilibrium

Mechanical or electronic models are simply great similar. The main highlights are to take a look at the equilibrium precision of something like 0.5 g and weight up to no less than 250 g, however, weight up to 1 kg is better. It should have adequately huge to weigh enormous size things.

Scapulae are utilized to slice and move agar and tissue cultures. Dispensable # 10 size surgical tool sharp edges are great for thin handling dissecting surgical blade cutting edges on the off chance that you can't find them, aluminum blade work, even though it very well may be somewhat challenging to rehearse in restricted spaces.

Inoculation circle

This wire circle toward the finish of a metal or wooden handle is utilized to change over a few spores or mycelium into agar plates. It very well may be viewed as in logical or brew-making stores or made of dowel and a piece of thin wire. An inoculation circle isn't needed on the off chance that you are using a cardboard plate system of spore germination.

Markers

These long-lasting, anyplace writing markers are fundamental for labeling a wide range of cultures.

Pipes

Having two sorts of plastic or metal pipes: a thin neck to hold fluid poring and largemouth channels to fill jars is useful.

Estimation [Serological) Pipette and Elastic Bulb

Assuming you intend to work with agar, you want to gauge in little amounts (1-15 ml) to add to your cultures. Pipettes measuring ten milliliters of glass are great for this reason since they can be autoclaved, reusable, and have markings to effectively set the volume. An elastic bulb is utilized to draw and disseminate the fluid from the pipette. Both can be found at logical suppliers and some blend stores. A glass 10 ml graduate cylinder or a bunch of metal spoons for measuring reason might be utilized, however, the work requires more consideration and handling and need the consideration to try not to contaminate your cultures.

Graduated Cylinder

They are utilized to precisely gauge fluids. Cylinders in liter, 100 ml, and 10 ml sizes should consider every contingency.

Measuring Cups and Spoons

Measuring cups and spoons can be utilized instead of graduated cylinders, however, are less exact — the Pyrex cups are 250 ml to 8 cups 2L volume, and metals for little volumes. At the point when sterilization is expected before use, the two sorts can be autoclaved or cleaned in boiling water for sterilizing for 5 minutes on a rolling bubble.

Syringe

For the mass spore inoculation procedure, syringes are utilized to inject. 10 ml or 20 ml sizes are utilized. They are utilized with to the max needles of 18 measures. They can be autoclaved in a tension cooker or cleaned in boiling water. Syringes can be bought at careful and veterinary stockpile stores and some online mushroom supply merchants. Be that as it may, their deals are customary in the US. Assuming you buy pre-filled spore syringes and needles, after utilize cleaning and getting the syringe and needle, they are required to have been autoclaved to be utilized again and again ordinarily Supplies;

Hydrogen Peroxide (3%)

Hydrogen peroxide (3%) is added to the cultures to forestall contamination. It is accessible at most drug stores or supermarkets. The positive retention of the hydrogen peroxide fluid in some cases varies, so ensure the packaged date isn't obsolete.

In this fixation, peroxide is generally innocuous to human health separated from wearing gloves, and no one-of-a-kind strategies are expected to deal with it. It is a gentle bleaching specialist, so be mindful not to toss it on garments. More focused (8 to 35%) arrangements are accessible from various sources, for example, pool supply stores and online. Hydrogen peroxide can cause serious aggravation in fixations over 3 and possibly consumes the focus more than 3%, so be extremely cautious.

Bleach

Standard power clothing dye is helpful for cleaning surfaces and apparatuses. Stay away from brands with additional cleansers. Weaken it to somewhere around 1% strength before use. The shower bottle having a 10% strength arrangement is incredible as a surface and air disinfectant.

Para-Film

Para-film is a paraffin-based, adaptable film used to seal Petri dishes. This gas is cracked, and that implies that it permits the trading of gases, keeping contaminations from cultures. A straightforward shape in 1-inch wide moves has been sold by some nursery providers as "grafting tape."

On the off chance that you can't find paraffin or Para-film, you can supplant polyethylene cling film, for example, Happy Wrap however not Plastic Wrap or comparable brands, which are made of polyvinylchloride and don't spill gas). Employing an extremely sharp blade (warily) cut a 1-2-inch broad segment toward the finish of the whole roll.

Careful Gloves

Dispensable plastic gloves are vital for getting wet hands far from your ideal culture. They needn't bother with to be disinfected ahead of time. Wash your hands and arms completely before putting gloves on, then, at that point, wipe the outside of the glove with a paper towel absorbed liquor (consistently dry them before going close to an open fire).

Substrate and Casing Material;

Entire Grain

For the planning of generating, the most regularly utilized substrate is entire grains. Entire grains make an optimal hotspot for produce for different reasons. Each grain goes about as a supplement, mineral, and water that is immediately colonized by higher organisms, while its sinewy husk shields it from being contaminated by different microorganisms yet to some extent. On colonization, the grains effectively separate from one another. Finally, when the frontier grain brought forth is utilized to inoculate mass substrates, each grain goes about as a reduced container of mycelium and supplement holds, a remote station from which the fungus can arrive at new mediums.

Albeit practically any oat grain goes about as a bring forth, it is suggested that delicate cold (white) wheat, as it has functioned admirably, and is liberated from sterile microbes containments that are available and grows on different grains. You might utilize anything grains are promptly accessible to you, although the proposed isn't huge grains like rye, wheat, or corn than little-grained grains, for example, millet or rice that can cluster together when cooked.

A few ranchers utilize wild birdseed blend that has given great outcomes and enjoys the obvious benefit of being modest and promptly accessible. In any case, since it is a combination of grains of various sizes, it is more challenging to accurately get it. It can likewise be very tacky when wet. To diminish these issues, absorb birdseed cold water for 24 hours and rinse and drain it completely before loading it into containers or containers. Whenever the situation allows, attempt to utilize natural grains, as this is the best way to ensure that they are not treated with pesticides or fungicides.

Malt Obtains and Dried

It is a powder removal that has been grown to some extent and converted into starch and sugar. Malt removal is utilized in agar media as a significant supplement asset. And afterward, it is to utilize the light or tan malt, the hazier malt is caramelized, and parasites don't grow well on caramelized sugar.

Yeast Concentrate

On the off chance that yeast separation is added to the agar media as a dietary enhancement, it is a dry concentrate of yeast cells plentiful in vitamins, minerals, and proteins. Brewer's yeast, accessible in numerous health foods stores, is an OK other option, although it isn't so compelling as yeast removal.

Calcium Carbonate (Cac03)

Calcium carbonate is likewise called lime, hydrated lime, limestone flour, clamshell flour, and chalk. Expanding the pH of soil and substrate, removing pollution, and providing calcium to growing soils are utilized. Parasites favor somewhat essential pH> 8 normal. Microscopic organisms and some other containment don't. Look at the mark to ensure the calcium carbonate you purchase has magnesium 1% off, as certain parasites don't blossom with the highly satisfying magnesium.

Calcium Sulfate

Calcium sulfate is known as gypsum, and calcium sulfate is utilized to catch more water in the substrates, making it simpler to shake up or isolate and to forestall water stagnation and contamination. It is unbiased in pH and doesn't can support.

Chips and Hardwood Sawdust

Chips and Hardwood sawdust are the substrates for mushroom species. Albeit the greater part is hardwood species, birch, cottonwood, oak, birch, and beech are great. Assuming you have one of the tree animal groups growing intently, you can get fresh chips from your Division of Interstates or nursery focus, or you can chip it for yourself. Chips produced using trees are best in winter or late winter, as they are high in sugar and have minimal verdant substances, which can be a vector for bed contamination.

In some cases, you can get hardwood chips locally from grill providers who sell them for food-smoking motivations. If you don't have entrée too locally hardwood, wood chips online can be purchased. Beech or maple fine wood chips are sold as creature beds, however, they are normally perfect to utilize alone yet should be blended with other huge chips or some likeness thereof.

Pellets Filled Sawdust

Wood is utilized to warm the house, particularly in wood ovens. They are made of sawdust, which is additionally compacted in little pellets. The high intensity produced during the making process makes it less sterile. At the point when absorbed warmed water, the sawdust is gained after pellet extension. This item is accessible at home heating providers and some tool shops. Oven pellets make an extraordinary wellspring of sawdust for substrates - simply make a point to get just a single brand, particularly produced using hardwood. They are additionally sold as fuel for food smokers in different tree species like birch and oak.

Dowels Twisting Notched

Dowels Twisting Notched is promptly accessible from woodworking providers, for example, furniture part providers, that the mushrooms utilize 1 to 2 inches long and 1/4 inch or 5/16 inch in measurement. They are generally taken from birch and are named in that capacity. They are usually utilized in the development of mushrooms on logs, where colonized dowels are crushed in openings around the logs. The twisting section on the external side of the dowel gives an enormous surface region from which the mycelium can hop into the following substrate.

Feline Litter Paper Pellet

Cultures in little glass tubes are utilized to store Feline Litter Paper pellets. The free surface and restricted supplements of the paper make it ideal for long-haul care of most mushroom species. Find a brand that isn't perfumed and has 100 reused papers.

The Peat Greenery

A piece of the shaped soil, peat greenery, is sold all over and in gardening places. Even though its dietary benefit is extremely low, its high water stockpiling limit gives dampness to developing organic product bodies. It is somewhat acidic and should be cushioned with calcium carbonate.

Vermiculite

Vermiculite is one more piece of dirt. It is utilized for its water stockpiling limit and its smooth, open design, which grants for appropriate gas trade. It is accessible to many nursery providers. Utilize the coarsest grades. There is a myth that vermiculite contains asbestos, which isn't substantial. Vermiculite and comparative ingredients, (for example, peat and calcium salts) contain fine particulates, which can be unsafe to inhale. Continuously wear a painter's residue cover while storing or handling them.

Water Gem

Synthetically made of an engineered polymer joined to super paste, these gems can absorb multiple times their mass in water, and afterward bit by bit drop water content in their surroundings. When completely hydrated, they seem to be unadulterated gelatin. They are utilized in agriculture and horticulture to hold water use and keep plants from drying out completely between the water. In mushroom development, they are added to the casing soil as it keeps up with appropriate dampness levels. Precious stones come in two sorts: those made of sodium and others from potassium. Since high sodium levels are hurtful to numerous growths, make a point to have assortments made of potassium.

Chapter 6

Psilocybin Culture Method

Mushroom food (otherwise called the substrate) is like edible human food: a healthful compound that adjusts carbs, proteins, minerals, and vitamins. Like our food, it is delectable to a wide assortment of miniature creatures, as a portion of bread forgotten about on a kitchen counter for more than a couple of days ends up being extremely fast. Likewise, dissimilar to people, parasites are miniature living beings and need to compete with some other microorganisms around. There is a competitive advantage of microscopic organisms and form, as they can imitate a huge number of times quicker than normal mushroom species may. Any substrate that has a single shape spore or a bacterium can turn out to be a rotten or mushy wreck.

Furthermore, room air contains more than 100,000 particles for every typical cubic centimeter. A covered-up, quiet shower of shape, dust particles, and even dust grains is continuously settling up each flat surface of your home, regardless of clean your thought process is.

The main way to deal with restricting these critters from hijacking mushroom cultures is to ensure they never assault them in any case. There are two fundamental means to do this: eliminate anything that any shape or microbes there, to begin with, and work in any spotless or sterile climate by excluding them. We eliminate contaminations and begin the sterilization process on issues them in the tension cooker, where any organic entity might get by under high temperature (1210 C/255 'F) and strain (15 PSI). By filtering the air in our working environment and sterilizing it with synthetic disinfectants.

Both of these strategies structure the method of disinfection or aseptic culture, which you want to gain proficiency with the main thing to find success in growing mushrooms. Repeating it to underscore the procedure of sterile culture, which is the main thing you can gain from this book. On the off chance that you don't comprehend this, no development techniques work, regardless of how intently you adhere to the instructions. On the off chance that you're lucky, you might grow one mushroom or two, yet generally, you have a shiny cluster of blue, green, and dark molds and a Stinky, malodorous gathering of microorganisms. Many expected mushroom growers have flopped wretchedly here, and the individuals who have succeeded have taken in the most difficult way possible how and why clean culture strategies can be utilized. We expect that the strategies depicted in this section give you simple ways, which save you a ton of time and sorrow.

Cleaning up your workspace is the principal errand to make a spotless spot. Preferably, you could commit a room or space just to your mushroom projects, like an extra room or an unused stroll in the storeroom. Assuming no such space is accessible, a normal size kitchen can do a ton of lab work, yet for that, you want to set up and maintain a cleanest and disinfected climate. The kitchen competes with the washroom to be the most complicated and naturally dynamic room in the house, and there are a ton of dynamic molds. Then again, working in the kitchen gives admittance to water sources and over the oven. Assuming that you intend to save various spaces for mushroom work, ensure it is near the kitchen.

It is a waste of time to disinfect and sterilize your issues to convey to your lab from the filthy house. The work area should have a very much estimated table, ideally one with a continuous, handily cleaned surface. Formica or lacquer is great, as the need might arise to wipe the workbench with liquor before each utilization. On the off chance that you have a wooden table, consider placing a thin piece of compressed wood with a piece of plastic laminate surface or a piece of thick vinyl alongside the outer layer of the piece of plastic when you work. Likewise, the work area floor should be not difficult to clean (linoleum or tile) and simple to clean. Carpets become an assortment of residue and spores. Millions are tossed into the air constantly and should be stayed away from if conceivable. The walls should be spotless (a fresh layer of paint won't be an issue), and different regions and surfaces in the room should be entirely cleaned. If, practically speaking, utilize a legitimate disinfectant arrangement.

Assuming you're working in your kitchen, you can't disinfect each surface each time you intend to utilize it, yet you can from opportunity to time premise profoundly clean it occasionally. Clean and disinfect however much as could reasonably be expected before each utilization. To downplay wind passing, the region around your culture should be liberated from drafts of air developments. Windows should be firmly shut, heating or cooling pipes should be covered, and entryways should be shut before work begins.

Eliminate different wellsprings of contamination from the room whenever the situation allows. Planted in pots, fish tanks, and pet food, trash, get take them out and discard them in the dumpsters. It additionally assists with operating an air filtration gadget in space. These days, appropriate air filtration gadgets cost not exactly $ 100, and they are calm and productive enough to reliably work. Ensure the unit you purchase is HEPA-evaluated. HEPA represents High Efficiencies Particulate Air. It has an authority channel rating, and that implies it gets particles 0.1 microns (1/100th piece of a millimeter) and bigger or 99.97% solids in the air. We keep our channels low consistently, and high for an hour before working in the lab to give air after filtering it.

Finally, you want to clean the air in your working region. You can do this by working inside a glove box, which is an encased space that can be completely disinfected and sans draft. Or on the other hand before a stream hood through an enormous HEPA channel unit that blows a constant flow of unadulterated, sterile air into your working space, excluding all contaminants. The glove box can be made rapidly and inexpensively, yet it is less productive, as the air can find its direction into the room. Stream hoods cost much more, however, the cash is generously compensated for, as it grants you to work in the open while as yet maintaining the aseptic procedure.

Taking Care of Private Cleanliness

Now that you've tidied up your space, now is the right time to think about one more fundamental wellspring of contamination in your transitory lab, and that is YOU. Your body, hair, and garments are an Amazon wilderness of microbes, infections, and growths, stowed away from your eyes and generally not unsafe to you or others, but rather dangerous to mushroom culture. To downplay this disgusting group, you should be as spotless as conceivable before each work meeting.

It implies taking a shower, drying with freshly cleaned towels, and preceding work. Wear a perfect arrangement of garments. Your decision on clothing is additionally fundamental. Try not to wear long-sleeved shirts or baggy garments that might tumble off during your work. If you have broadened hair, bind it back to your head. Clean and wipe your hands and lower arms with isopropyl, and rubbing liquor, and consistently wear dispensable careful gloves and wipe the beyond the glove with liquor while working.

Hygienic Mind

At the point when you set up your working environment and your body, ensure you include your mental state before you go to work. Mental cleanliness is pretty much as significant as private cleanliness because your mental state influences how you work, and on the off chance that you are hurried or in a rush, you commit an error or apply a pollutant to your culture. Your developments in the lab should be done cautiously, estimated, and purposely.

Stay away from pointless quick or insane developments, as they just make undesirable air flows. You take as much time as is needed. If you are in a rush, decelerate down or save the labor for a day when you have additional time. Likewise, ask your life partner, kids, dog, or feline not to upset you when you go into the room or at work and disengage the telephone. Play without a hitch, modern music on the off chance that you need it, however, stay away from speed metal except if you have any desire to loosen up your ears.

Keeping Records of Processes

It is crucial to have an entire and nitty gritty record of all tests or development processes or every one of the strategies which are best for any successful lab procedure. Most phases of mushroom development are more stretched out than previously and extend than the past working. For instance, on the off chance that each plate could be utilized to inoculate 10 new plates or 6 containers, each jug could inoculate

6 packs, etc. Making hundreds, even a great many individual cultures are simple. Having a method for identifying each culture rapidly and effectively save you a ton of time and exertion in the long run. Also, keeping its record cause you to find support from these records and moves significantly further to upgrade the task. It assists you with deciding on the advancement of your work, distinguishing victories and disappointments, and tracking it to assist you with reaching the source.

We record each culture pot in a coded numbering framework, and record lab work and code in a lab scratch pad. A scratch pad works, even though queuing or diagramed pages help separate from normal pages of information and create tables or pictures. On the off chance that the pages of the book are not currently numbered, add page numbers at the highest point of each page.

At the point when you make another arrangement of trials (for effortlessness, any individual culture container should be viewed as an examination), begin a clear page. At the highest point of the page, record the date and a note of what you explored different avenues regarding ("MYA plates" or "rye grain jolts") that contain pertinent information, for example, the utilization of restrictive recipes or surprising strategies are utilized. Since each starting culture is generally used to inoculate new ones, each trial can be gathered by putting a strong line after each last new culture, and consequently putting it in sections. Consequently, the original social information should be placed just a single time. The right-hand segment is utilized to record notes about each culture as it grows over the long haul. Put it down on the calendar for each note that is followed when passed. Aboriginal cultures are set apart with a similar name, using an indelible marker on the edge of the plate and beyond the container. It includes the species, strain code, and the bracket of original the instigating tests. Recording these total details is simpler.

Keep every one of the obligations finished after every one of the tests, at the same time in the day.

Chapter 7

The Grain Activity

Arranging the Grain Spawn

Grain spawnd is produced using entire grains, which contain a little amount of calcium carbonate and calcium sulfate. Calcium carbonate goes about as a pH cushion, while calcium sulfate keeps individual grains from sticking together. Both give mineral sustenance to the fungus. In any event, for appropriate cooking and sterilization, the grains are softly bubbled, doused for the time being in high temp water, drained, canned, and cleaned.

Many grain microscopic organisms can hinder the endospores. These exceptionally opposing designs are intended to persevere through outrageous environmental circumstances, which can forestall sterilization and drenching of the grains for the time being making the endospores grow. The intensity rapidly kills microscopic organisms and microbes.

Practically any natural, including wheat, rye, maize, and millet, produces natural entire grains. We utilize white (delicate) wheat in winter since it is not difficult to find, cooks well, and has low bacterial endospores.

1. Make sure to use an enormous pot since when the grain is cooked, it is two times the volume. Fill it with water something like two times as the need might arise, and afterward heat the pot in your oven. Be cautious while pouring in dry grain, and put the pot in a full rolling bubble.

2. Leave it there for ten minutes, switch off the burner, and let the pot sit for the smallest 8 hours (however not more than 16), yet it should be about two times the amount and hydrated satisfactorily. To check, crush the grain between your fingers, it should be exceptionally delicate on the inside.

3. Drain the water. Assuming that the grain is all tacky after the drain, rinse in a few times with cold water and drain again entirely.

4. Put the grains into the container with the necessary amount of calcium carbonate and calcium sulfate. Secure, shake well, and fill into the strain cooker, making sure to leave however much space as could be expected between individual containers. (Try to add a pipette or other autoclaved measuring containers to gauge your peroxide later.)

5. Sterile for a reasonable amount of time.

6. Let it cool for the time being completely before use. Leave the containers in a fixed strain cooker until prepared to inject.

Agar-To-Grain Move

Agar cultures are generally used to inoculate tiny grains into a quart-sized container. After which can be fruited or huge grain containers can be inoculated. One full colonized plate can be utilized to inoculate a limit of 6-quart containers. Peroxide is normally added to the grain at the hour of inoculating so 6 ml for each

2-3 cups of cooked grain can get extra insurance against contaminants.

1. Open the strain cooker and put every one of the containers in the glove box or stream hood.

2. Lose the front of each container without removing the cover, then, at that point, measure the necessary measure of H2O2 in each container, Lift and eliminate the cover using the other hand and eliminate the cover with your other hand, then firmly seal the container.

3. Completely separate the grains by shaking each container obviously to isolate the grains and spread the peroxide completely and equally, and afterward shake again aside the container. It leaves the grains on a lofty incline. Then lose the cover completely yet don't isolate it. Return the container to the working spot, and ensure the grains are not upset from the inside.

4. Do the indistinguishable strategy to the remainder of the containers.

5. In the process of transferring agar to agar, make a point to disinfect the blade and cool it in an unfilled agar plate (or let it cool gradually).

6. Now, open up the culture plate and cut it into pieces or wedges (minimum two for each pot). Try not to cut the original parent culture from the center of the plate.

7. Use the surgical blade to stick one cut wedge on the tip of your surgical tool, the cover, and close the plate. Then open it by removing the front of the primary container, and putting the agar wedge on the surgical blade at the lower part of the grains. It better is to put it where mycelium is available or mycelium side (contact the grain). You can tap the handle of the surgical blade outwardly edge of the container to isolate the wedge from the surgical blade assuming that you think it is fundamental, yet tenderly to prohibit contamination.

8. Do a similar process and rehash something very similar with different wedges, set the cover on the container back, and afterward do

generally a similar process by moving on to the following container.

9. Once every one of the containers has been finished, a similar process and have been inoculated. Straighten out their covers and tenderly tap back the inclined grains to entirely wrap the wedges of agar. Shaking the container at this stage isn't wise to do, albeit a large portion of the mushroom growing techniques has proposed doing it so. What we have found is that letting the mycelium first allow leaping off the agar wedge to the grains before shaking gives great consequences for healthy cultures.

10. Now name appropriately on the external side of the container with an indelible marker and put it in the working spot or into incubation.

Grain Syringe Inoculation

For grains and syringe inoculation, you can utilize the technique for PF-style spore water syringes for grain inoculation. Hydrogen peroxide can kill the spores; hence, it should not be utilized, other than that this process is basic.

1. Once the grains are disinfected, and the containers have been chilled off to the temperature of the room. Move them to the stream hood or the glove box.

2. The front of the containers currently perhaps relaxes yet don't eliminate them from the containers.

3. Use the syringe by removing the cover from the syringe and wiping the needle with a cotton ball absorbed liquor, and afterward further clean the needle by holding the tip of the needle into the fire of your liquor light until it warms up and begins to become red. Let it chill off for a couple of moments before using the needle of the syringe.

4. Open up the container once at a time to inject a few millimeters of spore suspension onto the grains slowly.

5. Cover the containers and seal them, then, at that point, mix them and put them for incubation.

Container Incubation

The containers, as you most likely are aware, have enormous sizes and have different and odd shapes, the incubator probably won't have adequate space to accumulate them all. Except if you have a few incubators previously installed, or need to make a few additional incubators, or install some other heating framework, you can simply keep the containers warm, without draft region, like a pantry shelf. However long the temperature is 65 to 80 F, they grow without having any additional intensity. If at low temperatures, they are somewhat delayed to grow. The mushroom mycelium that is effectively growing radiates heat as it uses the substrate. By and large, there is sufficient activity going on in the quart container that raises the temperature above the surrounding by a few degrees. Subsequently, it is smarter to commit errors. Simply be certain that they don't get more intense or get overheated. It better is to try not to keep containers where the temperature is over 80 degrees.

Shaking the Grain Jars

The grain cultures that are continually growing should be shaken occasionally to speed up the growth quickly and equitably. In a couple of days of the week after the inoculation process, mycelium should have leaped out of the wedges. Also, begin the colonization of the surrounding grains. When this expanding circle of mycelium arrives at an inch or more in breadth, shaking the jar is prepared. Gradually and delicately shake the jar to shake up the grain bunches and modify them. At the point when the jars become an ever-increasing number of pioneers, individual grains get appended by the mycelium and become challenging to separate. If you have any desire to utilize power to separate the obligation of the grains, don't utilize pat or tap the jar using the center of your hand or some other piece of your body.

Those Jars that are utilized now and again, particularly those that have gone through different processes of sterilization, may frequently have concealed pressure breaks and may break abruptly. Consequently, patting the jar using the center of your hand could give you an extreme injury. Instead of that, pat the jar on a thick however clean towel upheld by a strong cushion. You can utilize 2-inch channel tape put on a strong tabletop. The jar could be shaken two times when colonization is noticeable at 5% and afterward half, or once in seven days till the grain is completely gotten comfortable in the province. After the principal shake, the mycelium around the grains that are colonized is separated into practically inconspicuous parts. It might look like there is no life existing in the jar, yet in a little while, you should see the recuperation of the mycelium and begin growing province in the grains at many more spots than previously.

Grain Contamination

Investigate your grain jars and check whether there are any indications of contamination. Focus after shaking; most clearly, clean jars uncover stowed-away contamination following a few days. If the recuperation of mushroom mycelium isn't noticeable or gradually happening, it could be an indication of bacterial contamination. Bacterial contamination frequently appears as wet stamps or air pockets around the grain or on the inner surface of the jar. One more side effect of bacterial contamination is a foul smell like a spoiled apple or a harsh maturation scent. It tends to be checked by sniffing the jar through the channel. You can undoubtedly recognize pigmented spores that are an indication of form contamination.

While working with grain products, it is fundamental to isolate contaminated jars from the spotless ones that have no contamination at the earliest opportunity. The grain is so loaded with nourishment that a single shape spore can colonize a whole jar in days and make billions of spores in the process. Consequently, be mindful of the grounds that opening such jars would let these shape spores contaminate and spread in the whole space for quite a while. A few growers put these shaped spore-contaminated jars into the strain cooker to dispose of contamination and sanitize the items in the jars before they can spread across the room. While this can be overwhelming, you should discard contaminated grain and disinfect the contaminated jars before using them again, and before doing some other social work, ensure that you shower completely and clean the garments however much you could.

Relocating Grain to Grain

When the grain jars are colonized with healthy items, they should be at the earliest opportunity utilized, because the significance and ease of use spawn declines in your odds of coming out on top, following possibly 14 days.

You can utilize the little jars containing colonized grains to inoculate the new jars, either huge or little. Thusly, the little amount of inoculation spawnd can be grown to bigger amounts. A little jar can inoculate ten jars of comparable size at the greatest or four greater jars of a similar size, very much like produce sacks. Each produce age can be utilized to make one more jar for produce age, even though it is ideal to restrict such grain move to not over three bring forth ages to forestall strain senescence. Mind one thing that grain quart jars can be utilized to inoculate to fruiting substrates, or even to be fruited itself (P-Cubbins'). Consequently, the grain-to-grain move is just productive when you need to expand the no of brings forth.

For all number of jar cultures assortment, pick a few healthy examples for the move. In any populace of cultures, barely any cultures normally look healthier than others. Leave out any that show even the more modest indication of shortcomings, such as sluggish growth, wet spots, or grains that remain not colonized in the wake of shaking for various times. Shake the best-chosen jars again, allow them to incubate for a little while, and offer them one final chance to uncover themselves. Healthy cultures should be healthy as of now and recuperate, with each grain with mycelia growth. Some other outcomes should be dismissed on the off chance that not qualifying for health culture.

The exchange of Grain-to-Grain resembles agar movement, pretty much. After mixing peroxide into sterile grain containers, a modest quantity of colonized grain is added to them. The specific amount of produce that was added relies upon the number of new containers to be inoculated and should be isolated equally between them. Before using the new inoculated jars, they should be fixed, all around shaken, and named before incubation.

Sacks and Other Enormous Range Boxes

Many mushroom growers utilize autoclaved bring-forth sacks while making prepared more quarts. It is because of a few reasons. The single standard size of the pack can hold multiple times more grain than a single quart jar, and the sacks can occupy next to no room inside a strain cooker or incubating region.

The sacks are likewise adaptable and can let simple control and inspection of their items. It's off-kilter to shake a jar bigger than a quart, while the grains inside the sack can be effortlessly confined and revised.

Sacks can constantly be inoculated than jars or other huge grain containers, yet never from agar. You want an enormous amount and level of inoculums for each pack to rapidly settle contamination, in request to colonize the huge amount of substrate in the sacks.

One hindrance of using packs is that their enormous sizes make trouble keeping away contamination and maintaining sterilization. Indeed, even a single pack occupies a lot of room in a glove box, and it is exceedingly difficult to work with more than each in turn. For this, they are commonly inoculated inside the huge stream hood. Regardless of whether you approach the right stream hood, it is proposed to involve peroxide in other grain spawn sacks to safeguard them further. The motivation sealer is utilized to seal spawn sacks.

At the point when utilizing enormous spawn containers, sacks, or pots, forestalling the overabundance of clammy inside the container is fundamental. Little grain containers can get through a limited quantity of water in them. A couple of teaspoons of dampness, in the end, be gotten by the mycelium and may deal with no issue. With an enormous amount of grain, however, a such overabundance can increase rapidly. Aggregate dampness can obstruct the mycelium and go about as a vector for contamination. It is expected in no modest quantity of gypsum and calcium carbonate in the enormous containers.

There are many advances you might take to forestall excessively soaked culture containers. To begin with, don't overcook the grains. Furthermore, let the hydrated grains drain for a long time before use.

Finally, before sterilization, on the off chance that you set up your containers, they look extremely wet; add some additional gypsum to ingest over the top dampness. The grain that is satisfactorily arranged is dry to the touch, yet these grains keep some dampness still inside. It is particularly fundamental while preparing grain sacks, which obtain more peroxide than containers, due to the increases in the gamble of contamination.

Cooking and Loading Packs of Grain

1. After the sacks are filled, crush out all the extra air from the pack, and crease the fold back

and under the pack, leaving the channel piece facing outside.

2. Place the sack in the strain cooker in such a success that the channel patches are remained uncovered. They are leaving however much space as could be expected between the sacks. Utilize a liner or trivet to get the sacks from the lower part of the cooker, and particularly make a point to watch out. They don't contact the outer walls; otherwise, they dissolve. In the case of using peroxide, pack the graduated pipette or cylinder. Include the perfect proportion of water to the tension cooker and strain cook for 2.5 hours having 15 PSI. Add how much water to the boot cooker and strain cooker for 15 to 2.5 hours.

1. Once totally cooled, move the packs to your work area.

2. Shake the culture jar to isolate the grains that are colonized inside.

3. Take 80 ml of peroxide, open a pack rapidly, put peroxide in it, and close the fold to keep out flying contaminants. By folding the fold of the pack in certain layers and holding it firmly, shake the sack daintily to completely convey peroxide and leave the sack shut in your work area.

4. Do the indistinguishable technique to the remainder of the packs.

5. Individually open each pack, add the expected measure of colonized grains, overlap back the fold, and do likewise with the remaining sacks.

6. Use a drive sealer to seal each sack and swipe two times the pack for sealing, then, at that point, that would be smart.

7. Shaking the pack well is a brilliant thing to do and afterward mark the external side of every one of the sacks with definite and significant information on it.

It is referenced before that rising parasitic cultures produce temperature as they consume substrate. With numerous enormous containers, the increasing temperature can be sufficient, and it is fundamental not to allow the temperature to overheat during incubation. In this way, let it incubate someplace in a generally cool spot, someplace in the temperature scope of 65-75 degrees. Packs should never be touching one another. Leave a more than adequate space of no less than 4 inches around every one of them with the goal that the air dissemination is adequate and a lower temperature is maintained.

Chapter 8

Learning the Agar Activity

The arrangement of Agar Plates for mushroom culture is by and large maintained on sustenance agar plates. The level, semi-strong surface delivers a spiral, twofold growth design, a culture can be effectively tried, and any contamination should be recognized and separated. There is a polysaccharide, a sugar particle that is found in some cell walls of green growth. At the point when scattered in boiling water and afterward chilled, agar to some extent hardens, like gelatin. Agar fungus itself gives no sustenance to the growths, a few supplements are added to the medium, for example, malt sugar and yeast separate.

The ingredients are blended in with water in an intensity-resistant container, cleaned in a tension cooker, and filled with Petri dishes in a fluid state. One of the most utilized media is malt yeast extricate agar or a.k.a. MYA. It is an intentional medium on which a wide range of mushrooms cheerfully grows.

Senescence and Process

Growers frequently utilize elective media to keep away from the Senescence strains that are social corruption brought about by the aging process. At times after a few exchanges in the plates, a culture might begin to grow with feebly or even quit growing at last. The Senescence cultures are having either blemished natural products or have not in any way shape or form. It is generally left for isolating again from the intense strains and spores. The reasons for the senescence strains are as yet not surely known, however it frequently happens when a culture is maintained on the media recipe of the ideal opportunity for quite a while. Organisms truly do well when they are served different foods, and like us, they get exhausted and kick the bucket when they are taken care of the same thing consistently. To keep away from

Senescence, it's critical to separate each time you utilize your media solution, which "works out" the fungus, and the difficulties the different fungus catalysts establish at each point in time. An easy method for performing this is to add a little grain flour to each bunch, changing the sorts you are using each time you trickle in the new plates.

Some of the time, however, you need to challenge your fungus, significantly more, to allow it to grow further. It helps in reviving the culture that started to show indications of shortcomings. In this case, you need to eliminate every one of the normal sugars and starches and give it a total oddity to process. It might grow gradually on another medium, however following half a month of improvement, when you move it to a reasonable medium like MYA, it is probably going to detonate with growth.

What to take care of, is any cellulose, starch, or sugar, including soybeans, paper pellets, raspberry jam, and peanut butter. Whichever you think serves best. We have his likewise known about a rancher fungus dry cricket he got from a pet store! Sometimes, you might find material on which your fungus will not grow. Assuming this is the case, no issue, simply have a go at something else. One more method for avoiding strains of corruption is to lessen the number of changes in each culture. Instead of creating another variety each time you want another culture, make bunches of duplicates of the prior breeds, and put away them for some time in the future.

1. After watering, add all dry parts to the jar. Try to utilize a jar that is 1.5 to 2 volumes expected by the media, so it doesn't bubble during sterilization. Plug the neckline of the container with cotton fleece, and afterward wrap the neck with aluminum foil.

2. Place the jar in a strain cooker with the necessary measure of water. If you are adding peroxide to the agar, make certain to disinfect

a couple of sets of puppets enveloped by aluminum foil to oversee sterilization before use.

3. Sterilize for 30 minutes to 15 PSI pressure. Try not to cook your agar media for over 45 minutes, as it can make the media caramelize and organisms can't grow better in caramelized sugar.

4. Allow the tension cooker to come to climatic strain, and afterward cautiously place the jar and pipettes in the glove box or front of a stream hood during the intensity. It is useful to utilize a few layers of clean paper towels as a potholder as transferring things from pressure cookers to the working region.

5. When using peroxide: when endured outwardly of the jar sufficiently agreeable to deal with yet warm (between 120- - 140 ° F), using a sterile pipette or measuring spoon, add 8 ml of 3% hydrogen peroxide. Gradually pivot the medium a few times in the two bearings to blend well. Be mindful so as not to over-shake

as it makes bubbles, which wind up in your plates.

1. The opening front of Petri dishes is named on the packaging, and stacking those on the right side reveals your Petri dishes for some time in the future.

2. They are using the stacked dishes most extremely 10 all at once and afterward lifting all stacks in a single hand by the front of the base plate. Leaving the base half on the highest point of the seat, and putting sufficient medium into the dish to cover it completely by replacing the stack and rehashing it with the plate over it. For the Petri dishes of 100mm and with 20-30 dishes, one liter of the medium is sufficient. Try not to attempt to over-shake the blend while dripping the medium. On the off chance that there are components in the lower part of the jar, leave them there. Any suitable sustenance components should be available in the arrangement and medium in your dishes to be spotless enough and straightforward.

3. If you feel that agar began to solidify before adding water, it assists with keeping the jar in a somewhat hot pot (150 water F) while not using.

4. Place the whole plates in a section, and supplant the covers freely so that each plate can cool gradually and uniformly, reducing the focus on the upper plates. (They can become vectors for contamination). This impact can be accomplished by covering each stack with a portion of a spotless cup of warm water.

5. Permit the plates to get cool down for the time being.

6. The peroxide plates can be left in a virus-sans draft place for a few days to eliminate further focus. Place them in a few stacks, somewhat covered with clean sheets of paper. Plates without peroxide should be set in the covers when it cools.

7. Slide the plastic sleeve back onto the plates and wrap it firmly with clear packing tape. Store

the agar however keeping side-ups (to diminish buildup) and keep it in a cool, dry spot until required again.

Caring for Petri Dishes and Culture

While transferring, the cover should be taken out in a short time as could be expected — and put on the straight over of the plate to ward contaminants off.

Cultures should be put away agar on the potential gain. Be that as it may, it is smart to broaden the new exchange a day or so before reversing it to the new plate, or the exchange material may not remain on the new agar surface. Culture plates should be folded over their edges with a few layers of Para-film. To grow such mushrooms or gather new examples from the wild, you want to begin with cultures from spores to isolate your culture from unadulterated fruiting strains. There are two methods for starting a mushroom culture from spores on agar. In the conventional strategy, a sterile inoculating circle is utilized to take a few spores from a print, and afterward maneuver it into the agar plate. Recall that you can't utilize peroxide contained Petri dishes for this reason as it kills the spores.

On the other hand, on clean cardboard circles, spores are germinated; this strategy offers a wide range of advantages over the traditional procedure. The tiny size of the plates and the tight openings in the test tubes assist with keeping containments from cultures that are presented to peroxide. Moreover, it is a rapid framework: the circles are immediately colonized and afterward put straightforwardly on the peroxide agar. Ultimately, since the plate fills in as a substrate and a device to raise spores from a spore print, it gives for an exceptionally capable exchange, which is particularly useful when the spore print is oblivious and in the light.

By using the cut openings, little circles are cut with thin, level cardboard (dark sheets are right on the rear of the paper cushions). They are marginally dampened, put in a jar, and disinfected with test tubes too that contain 5-10 drops of malt yeast remove arrangement. At the point when cooled, the circles can be utilized to channel a few spores, and afterward drop into a cylinder, where they absorb the malt arrangement. Over the long haul, the spores germinate, and when the little circles become completely colonized into peroxide agar plates, they are moved.

Propagation of Agar Spores

This strategy is lined up with the one utilized while making spore water syringes, then again, actually the spores are moved into sans peroxide agar plates instead of water.

1. In your stream hood, heat the inoculation circle in a liquor light until it becomes red while heating.

2. Lift the front of the main Petri dish with your direction; pressing the finish of the circle to cool in the center of the agar (this likewise shapes a

thin movie of agar on the circle that can assist the spores with sticking).

3. Cover the plate and afterward utilize the circle to get a few spores from your print.

4. In an S-shaped movement streak across the Petri dish and afterward close it.

5. Again, sanitize the plates and cool the circle before splashing each plate.

6. Wrap the edges with Para-film, after inoculation, splash the plate, mark them with any information, and with the side up incubate agar.

Cardboard Plates Propagation

1. Put the cardboard plates in a pint jar with 1-2ml of water and seal it. Put 5-10 drops of malt arrangement in a test tube and a little seal. Sanitize and disinfect jars and cylinders for 15 min on 45 PSI and grant to cool.

2. Keep all devices and equipment in your glove box or stream hood.

3. Use a liquor light to warm the tweezers until hot and afterward cool them.

4. Use the tweezers to eliminate the circle from the jar and afterward cover the jar.

5. To the piece of the spore print, softly contact the edge of the circle. You should have the option to see the shining dark spores with the circle.

6. Place the circle at the lower part of the cylinder in the wake of opening a test tube.

7. Repeat the process 3-5 times for every cylinder.

8. For every spore print, make something like two plates.

9. Seal and incubate the cylinders with Para-film.

10. Move a few circles to isolate peroxide-added agar plates, when the spores are germinated, and the circles become completely colonized.

Incubation and Cloning

For incubation, which is a warm and sans draft place, keep at the temperature of 75-85° F, and keep the inoculated culture plates and spore circles. On the off chance that your home temperature stays within this reach forever, keeping it in a spotless box gets the job done. On the off chance that not, an incubator guarantees a superior and quicker states process. New, sterile mushrooms, either obtained from a complex spore culture or formed from the wild, may likewise be utilized to initiate agar culture. In this case, the ensuing culture should have a single strain and should show similar characters as connected with the initiating ones.

Since it is hereditarily like the strain from which it was isolated, it is viewed as a clone, and this technique is known as cloning. Along these lines, we by and large search for healthy examples to clone the populace, hoping to seclude this strain that furnishes dependable and energetic organic products with each utilization. Great quality to search for in the parent includes fresh, enormous, or thick foods grown from the ground characters that look healthy in general.

Separating a single strain that is fruiting is as simple as choosing the best examples from your harvests and culturing them on agar. The mushrooms are cut into a glove box or stream hood, and a little piece of clean mycelium is withdrawn from the spot of the cup situated on a fresh agar plate. After a short incubation period, a few bits of mycelia have grown out on the plate and afterward can be sub-cultured.

In any case, frequently, for no obvious explanation, clones got from similar guardians show various qualities of mycelia. Consequently, we make numerous cultures from each and save the best rich cultures because of the following use. Seems to be misleading and strains can't be anticipated by their appearance, so we clone whatever number of various examples as could reasonably be expected, permitted when and space to expand long-haul achievement. Since they were never uncovered from the outside climate, the cells on the inner side of the mushroom should be sanitized.

To ensure sterility, you should clone mushrooms quickly, even after picking the mushrooms. If you can't utilize them right now, you can place them in the refrigerator to store them in a clean Tupperware box with a fresh paper towel for a couple of days, yet at the same not excessively lengthy. Conversely, the peroxide in the agar media increases your possibilities of effective cloning, as it gives an additional layer of security from contaminants. Subsequently, we unequivocally suggest per-oxidized agar whenever you truly do tissue culture, except if you see that the species or strains don't endure it.

Tissue and Agar-To-Agar Move (Subculture)

1. Any free wet case matter should be completely cleaned before using the mushrooms for cloning. Assuming it is logical, this work should be avoided in the workspace.

2. Clean the mushroom outside surfaces with cotton ball-absorbed liquor, ideally while working in your glove box or stream hood.

3. Sterilize and clean the surgical tool in the liquor light, by holding the mushroom and gradually crushing the mushroom between your thumb and finger. You should have the option to separate it along the focal line, and afterward, if conceivable, strip the two parts of the mushroom along the length. If it's a tiny example, or not effortlessly analyzed, you can utilize a surgical blade to open it instead. Try not to slice with the blade to connect with the area you need to clone, as this can contaminate the external surface of the mushroom in your culture.

4. Disinfect the sharp edge again after each utilization.

5. As your Petri plate is prepared, cut a tiny piece of mycelium from the region of the stem or cap (typically in the thickest, most reduced region). The part should be pretty much as large as could be expected, in a perfect world. 3-8 mm wide and long. You should be mindful so as not to cut the upper surface and not disinfects the area of mushrooms in a manner.

6. Take a little piece of mycelium on the tip of your surgical tool. Lift the front of the Petri dish, put this piece on the focal point of the agar, and afterward close the plate. Once in a while, the stringy person of the mycelium can make it to join to the tip of the sharp edge. Assuming this is the case, attempt to cut this piece and push it down into the agar.

7. Repeat the equivalent with at least three plates for each mushroom.

8. Seal the plates with Para-film, mark them appropriately, and put them in the incubator. Keep them on the correct side up until they begin to grow, and afterward, bring them back to the ordinary.

You should see improvement in a couple of days of the week. From the outset, the piece is equally hazy, as the cells begin to part again. In the end, the mycelium arises out from where it associates the agar with the entire plate for colonization. At the earliest opportunity, the healthy cultures become sub-cultured, using just sterile mycelium from the edge of new growth, as the original tissues might cover stowed-away contaminants.

To move from one agar to another, a little piece of mycelium that looks healthy from the edge of the culture is cut with a sterile surgical blade placed in the focal point of another plate. Growing cultures or subcultures might be utilized within 1 cm of the edge of the plate before the appearance of the mycelium, as there might be contamination on the external edges of the plates, leading to numerous Secret containments under the mycelia advance front, just emerging upon the change to another medium.

If culture has an unadulterated strain, any piece of the rising edge can be a subculture. If it is a various strain culture (culture arising from multi-sport injection), you might need to pick mycelium with the favored qualities.

The presence of at least two mycelia species in a similar single culture is known as sectoring. The presence of healthy strain contrasts in some way or another from one specie to another, yet thick, rhizomorphic growth is a decent indication of general health for a wide range of mushroom species.

Stay away from areas that are growing mycelium unstable looking and slow-growing, which are not producing natural product strains. While transferring, consistently place the agar face of the pot on the drawback on the new plate. It does two significant things. In the first place, it opens the mycelium to coordinate contact with the agar, promoting quick colonization of the new plate. Second, by pushing the mycelium between the two layers of peroxide-containing agar, allowing any contaminated cells or microbes concealed on the mycelia surface to be exterminated.

Moves Agar to Agar

1. In a stream hood or glove box, it is smarter to dispose of any layer from an external perspective of the healthy culture bowl.

2. Heat the surgical tool cutting edge in your liquor light until it consumes then cools it in another Petri dish.

3. Grab the front of the original culture dish a bit and cut agar and mycelium in the ideal segments from ½ to 1cm in width. You can cut more than each wedge in turn.

4. To exchange, dispose of the top of the original culture plate. With a blade in one hand,

lift the front of the spotless plate marginally aside, place one wedge of agar medium from the culture plate to the tip of the blade and spot it in the center of the new plate, where the mycelium is on the drawback.

5. Replicate on every one of the plates, stamp, and imprint appropriately, and put in the incubator, as expected topsy turvy. (The cuts of agar stay with fresh agar, permitting the plates to be improved on the double.)

Contamination Assessing the Wellspring

Contamination is an unquestionable requirement in mushroom growing. One of the upsides of working with a two-way surface of agar plates is that the contaminating specialists are handily noticed and are let be from healthy or fit cultures. Contamination should dispose of from the developing region and squander on the double.

Infrequently, there might be a need to attempt to "save" a contaminated culture (on the off chance that you generally make a ton of reliable exchanges and maintain a spotless work routine, such conceivable outcomes should be interesting). You should constantly remove culture to new plates from contamination. Attempting to eliminate the contaminants from the agar plate by cutting the assailant off the plate, you are logical just to grow more contamination. As the shape spores are not difficult to be aggravated, it is hard to keep the contamination from transferring to your culture as well as to new plates, and there can be many exchanges before they are altogether eliminated. You can frequently find the wellspring of the contamination on agar by looking at the contamination design on the plate.

1.Contamination appeared before the utilization of plates. It could be an indication of insufficient sterilization of agar, inferior sterilization strategy during dripping or storing of the plates, or absence of peroxide fixation in the medium.

2. If there are indications of contamination on the edges of the plate, either single provinces or full rings, this might be an indication of that non-sterile air was brought into the plates when it was cooling down. To stay away, permit the agar to cool completely before inserting, and cover the plates with the plastic sleeves on the double after filling.

3. Contamination starting at the injection point is either an indication of a contaminated parent culture or inadequate sterilization of the surgical tool or injection circle. Notice cultures and the exchange mindfully before using cultures and try not to utilize the cultures assuming any uncertainty is available. Continuously keep the inoculating instrument warmed until red.

4. The contamination of microbes appears as thin, shiny, and straightforward, round states, frequently white, pink, or yellow. The microbes grow in moist conditions and extend rapidly to plates that have a high thickness on the top. Continuously hold on until the agar cools

enough before dripping, permit the plates to cool down leisurely in their plastic sleeves, and put them on the agar side up.

Strain Storing for Long haul

When you seclude the strain that spreads healthy fruiting strain, you can continue to spread a similar strain for quite a while, so you don't need to continuously rehash the process of disengagement. Continued cloning from one plate to another, and again and again at last make senesce of the strains, regardless of whether you change the technique for all time, as we recommended.

In this manner, consistently use cultures that have minimal exchange. You need to make an "originating" culture of any strain, which you respect for spreading when you remember it. The originating culture is then put away in the cooler for storing as long as possible and does likewise to the subcultures depending on the situation.

Put away cultures that are kept at a normal cooler temperature (38° F) enter a state of suspended versatility and can be established again by storing them in a fresh plate. Shortly after recuperation, the culture begins to ordinarily grow.

It is prescribed to store the culture in sterile paper pellets in test tubes. Because of the great sugar content of the media, the strains put away on the agar can end with noticing. Paper is low in supplements, to keep the culture healthy for quite a while. The tight entry of the test tubes is appropriate for minimal thickness and harmfulness, and their tiny mass lets for secure capacity. In any case, if you lack any admittance to the test tube, you can utilize a ½ pint bricklayer container or another equivalent little container that can likewise be autoclaved.

The cylinders should be put in optional jars after the culture is moved and allowed to grow, (for example, a zippered sack) and set in the fridge for capacity. This kind of strain can keep going for a long time, however, it's smart to gather the culture on each plate occasionally (more than once per year), and afterward sub-culturing and move to the plate, then, at that point, to paper for storing further. The impacts of peroxide are not surely known in cultures for long-haul stockpiling, so we get it far from our capacity media.

The Capacity Medium of Paper Pellets

1. Wet the paper pellets for field limit.

2. Load some into tubes. You want to remain cautious not to eliminate any bits of the medium external the cylinders. Freely seal it.

3. Put the jars in the tension cooker and keep a sterile at 15 PSI for 30 minutes. The containers can be stacked in layers, while the cylinders can be put in a rack or metal to keep them situated upward.

4. When the cooker is gotten back to ordinary gaseous tension but is yet hot to the touch, open it and cautiously move the containers to

your glove box and keep it there to get cool down for quite a while.

As Petri dishes, paper pellet tubes are additionally injected similarly. Since cultures don't have peroxide, and they will generally be put away for longer times, you require taking extra well-being measures to forestall the spread of contamination by following standard insurance rehearses. Likewise, at whatever point you open it, you should disinfect the neck of the inclined cylinder each time it is opened, wrapping it in the fire of your liquor light.

1. By fire, clean the neck of the open tub, and surgical tool.

2. Cut a tiny piece of agar from an influential culture, and put it in the sawdust tube. Since the neck of the test tube is excessively close to arriving at the blade, hold the cylinder on a level plane, make a cut on the top mass of the cylinder, seal it, and afterward delicately tap it on the sawdust.

3. Seal the container, wrap the cap or cover it with a Para-film band, and imprint it fittingly.

4. Until the paper is entirely colonized up till then incubate, then put the cylinders in another jar, for example, a cooler sack or Tupperware container, and make it refrigerated.

To recuperate the culture from the capacity container, place the culture at room temperature for 48 hours, and move a little piece of paper covered with mycelium from the capacity container to a fresh, agar Petri dish with the presence of peroxide.

Chapter 9

Containers for Fruiting and Casing Soil

After having total colonized substrates, you need to keep it in a container reasonable to case and fruit. Your chosen container relies upon the number of substrates that make up the fruit and can go from a little aluminum foil bread dish to a huge plastic bin. At the point when your fruit is in a little amount of grain, you should focus on a substrate that has a profundity of 2-3 inches.

Notwithstanding the size, a few highlights should be thought about while selecting a fruiting container. That should be made of a matter which is sufficiently hard to hold the substrate while colonization set up, letting to restrict how much light just on the dirt. Moreover, the absolute profundity of the container should be not beyond twofold the substrate profundity to allow secure gas to trade, while opening the container for misting.

A few growers utilize profound, totally shut containers with Snap-on covers, for example, plastic capacity bins to make a moist climate. Even though it works, it requirements to cut or bearing openings in the sides of the container to give gas trade, and this implies that the top should be straightforward so that light falls on the outer layer of the container. Instead, we like to utilize little, strong containers that are kept in the wet, giving the perfect proportion of light to the growing and fruiting chamber. The fruiting chamber should be straightforward as a perfect plastic sack that permits the trading of gas put close to a window of daylight, or as mind-boggling as a complex shelf unit beyond what one container can be put with sufficiently bright and humidifier.

The two kinds of fruit containers that are utilized for the most part are plastic tubs, which can contain 4-8-quart jars or a pack of grain, or a lot of substrates. For a more significant number of substrates, plastic bins are utilized. Little tubs are sold at equipment and kitchen supply stores, and plastic bins can ordinarily be bought at eatery supply distribution centers. Continuously utilize dull, thick containers to shield the substrate from the superfluous openness of the light.

Dampness and Moistness

The containers should be kept in a damp climate to stay away from quick dampness loss from the casing and substrate. Mushrooms require various degrees of stickiness; some need dampness level from 90% - 100 percent, though different necessities greatest 70% moistness. To the extent that the container is all around kept in an adequate number of more modest spots and the dirt is very much watered, the amount of water induces in the climate to keep mushrooms blissful and growing. Little tubs can be immediately enveloped by a perfect plastic sack. Cut in the top and sides of the sack should be penetrated or sliced to permit gas trade, four or five ½ inch openings for each square foot. (Numerous online mushroom providers sell pre-drill sacks for this reason.) To scatter the carbon dioxide from the case, they should be eliminated from the pack while misting. The packs should be adequately huge to help up to 8 inches of growing mushrooms from the dirt casing. Huge single containers can be set inside super clean plastic stockpiling tubs, penetrated around for gas trade, or put on a went-to-shelf unit. Such racks are promptly accessible online and available to be purchased. When joined with a planned lighting framework, they make extraordinary self-contained mushroom growing racks. Every shelf can have a few little containers or tubs, with mushrooms growing in the focal point of every shelf, with adequate space between shelves.

Mugginess Level

The little fruiting containers are set in penetrated plastic sacks. The single enormous container into huge sacks or tubs, and afterward these different bigger packs should be put on the racks.

However long the size of the dampness chamber intently matches the number of substrates it has, it should be not difficult to maintain the dampness level by hand misting on more than one occasion per day. At the point when the dirt is all around flooded, it should get water promptly to keep the mushrooms cheerful growing in the climate. If the air in your producing region is mostly dry, you might require another humidification framework.

Lightning Arrangement

The arrangement of your lighting should likewise be satisfactory and suitable for your growing region. Certain mushrooms don't take light like plants yet utilize light as an energizer for growth. A decent decision is that on the off chance that the spot is sufficiently bright to see around, that is sufficient. It should uphold the fruiting process finely. A few jars or single tubs require quite a sun-facing window or great surrounding light. More gigantic growing racks require an inherent lighting framework. Maybe 15-20-watt conservative luminous bulbs work dependably and utilize almost no energy. Nonetheless, they should be set external to the growing chamber to decrease heat and diminish the gamble of electrical short circuits. The size and amount of pots might be important to install lights in different areas to try not to create shaded areas on cultures. Electric lighting frameworks should likewise have clocks that need to illuminate the region for 8 hours every day.

Casing Soil Guidelines

Numerous assortments of grown mushrooms, including Psilocybin mushrooms, bear full fruit when the substrate is covered with casing soil. Casing soils are normally made out of non-supplement components with high water-absorbing limits, for example, gypsum and calcium carbonate with peat greenery and vermiculite. The casing soil layer carries out a few crucial roles in growing mushrooms. Because of the great water content, this layer keeps the substrate from losing dampness in the climate. It delivers a soggy miniature climate in which fragile primordia can shape, and goes about as a water repository for parched mushrooms as they grow.

Since the casing layer grows and delivers water like a wipe, it allows a grower to maintain the bed at its most extreme dampness level effectively as well as decreases the gamble of water-logging the substrate and fungus drowning. Additionally, the dampness level is more obvious on the particulate casing layer than on the exposed colonized substrate, which improves the humidifying process. Specific casing soil contains minerals like chalk and gypsum. Peat greenery is fairly acidic, and mushroom mycelium frequently supports the acidic compounds as it grows. Since exceptionally acidic conditions can be unsafe to organisms and invigorate bacterial growth, the expansion of chalk (calcium carbonate) to the dirt maintains a somewhat vital climate (pH b/w 7.5-8.5). Gypsum (calcium sulfate) is added to maintain a free, ventilated structure and to give mineral nourishment to growing growths in the type of calcium and sulfur.

The purported "water gem" is a discretionary part that you can add to your dirt blend. Artificially produced using super paste engineered polymers, these precious stones can retain up to multiple times their mass in water, and afterward leisurely release it around them.

When completely hydrated, they seem to be unadulterated gelatin. It is utilized in agriculture and horticulture or gardening to diminish water use and to monitor plants against drying out completely among watering lengths. Essentially, adding a few water gems to the dirt layer help to keep it hydrated and decrease the requirement for reliable misting. A single flush of mushrooms can deny the dirt and substrate of a huge amount of water, and these precious stones can give an extra degree of guarding to your cultures from drying out.

Albeit these are manufactured substances, water precious stones have been checked and viewed as non-harmful and environmentally agreeable. Over the long run, they retain completely carbon dioxide and water. They have been deductively tried for use in mushroom development and viewed as protected. Button mushrooms (Agaricus Bisporus) growing in their presence were seen not to corrupt the substance parts of the gel. Precious stones come in two sorts: those produced using sodium and others from potassium. Since elevated degrees of sodium are damaging an excessive number of organisms, try to have the sort from potassium. Since when the gems rot when warmed, they should be added to the dirt after sterilization or pasteurizing.

Albeit a few growers have suggested disinfecting the casing soil before using it to decrease contamination, as long as the equipment is kept perfect and dry, it is viewed as excessive. Nonetheless, if you need to be more cautious or you find that you generally disapprove of the contamination in your casing soil, quick assistance can be obtained from sterilization. A simple approach to pasteurizing a modest quantity is to utilize a microwave. Place the wet, readymade casing soil in an intensity-resistant container or sack (huge stove packs, how turkeys are cooked, or weighty plastic cooler packs are great) and pass on it to have a weighty microwave for around 15 minutes. Make certain to leave the sack or container open to keep it from exploding. Allow the pack to sit for 10 minutes, then place it in the microwave for an additional 15 minutes. If you don't contain a microwave, you can likewise disinfect it in a tension cooker for 45 minutes at 15 PSI, or prepare it at 3500 stoves for 2 hours. Allow it to cool totally before use. You might require adding strengthening water to bring the casing soil back to the ranch limit, as a portion of the dampness should lose after heat.

You here introduced three casing soil guidelines so you can get an understanding of the using the varieties, and you can undoubtedly exploit the substance accessible. Be that as it may, it is favored the Unadulterated Vermiculite recipe in light of multiple factors. First off, it's simple.

It is a lot more straightforward to eliminate coarse vermiculite from the foundation of grown mushrooms than from other casing ingredients. Vermiculite is created from a high-intensity process, so it is flawless, primarily rebellious to contamination, and needn't bother with to be sanitized before use. Most tellingly, because vermiculite is an inorganic substance, it gives no supplements to the fungus. Subsequently, it structures "overlay," a circumstance where casing grows the mycelium over colonized and binds firmly together seldom happens when it is utilized.

Note: Heaved vermiculite dust is extremely unsafe for the lungs. For well-being and security, the painter's residue cover should be worn while opening and working with it interestingly. When the vermiculite is damp, it quits dusting and is at this point not hazardous.

Unadulterated vermiculate Casing Soil (Course Vermiculate, Gypsum, Chalk)

Peat Greenery Casing Soil (Peat Greenery, Gypsum, Chalk)

50/50 Blend Casing Soil (Peat Greenery, Course Vermiculate, Gypsum, Chalk)

In every one of these guidelines, you can add ½ teaspoon of water gem per liter or casing soil quart. Continuously include them after any particular intensity therapy. Regardless of which adaptation you determine to utilize, the readiness method is equivalent to that utilized in other mushroom-growing procedures to convey the material to the field limit. Albeit colonized substrates and casing soils are less contaminated than the beginning phases of their growth, it is constantly amazing to remember to have on gloves and keep your work area, apparatuses, and containers as perfect as could be expected.

1. Thoroughly combine all ingredients well as one in a liquor-cleaned container.

2. Save 10% on this combination.

3. Add water to the rest until it is splashed, and you begin looking for free running water a few seconds ago.

4. Add back saved dry combinations. On the off chance that the well is soggy, squeezing a small bunch of soil can deliver a couple of drops of water. Sterile or purify it if necessary, and let it go altogether cool. Examine the example to be certain it is adequately wet and add water if necessary.

5. If wanted, include water gems.

6. Apply the casing to the substrate a couple of an at once, however much as could reasonably be expected. To keep the construction open and breezy, forestall packing it down. The profundity of the final layer might be from ½ inch to 1 inch.

After the casing layer is applied, the container should be without a moment's delay put under fruiting circumstances. Fog the container delicately and frequently and utilize a hand sprayer by mixing 0.3% of peroxide arrangement with 1 piece of 3% H_2O_2, blended in with 9 pieces of water, and regard it however much as could reasonably be expected.

The water needs of the fungus, during the casing colonization stage, are low, and spraying on more than one occasion per day should be sufficient to switch water loss. Be mindful so as not to splash water too enthusiastically or profoundly. It is ideal to splash the water gently and frequently on the casing soil layer, instead of soaking everything simultaneously, which isn't wise to do. The mycelium before long begins to go through the casing layer and emerge from the thinner casing layer than others. By using the perfect spoon, fix these spots by applying a wet amount of casing soil, with the goal that the whole layer runs equitably across the colonization.

Overlay

It is normally best to assume that the primordia developed somewhere inside the casing layer instead of on top of it to forestall the overlay issue. The overlay happens when the vegetative mycelium is allowed to colonize the total casing layer, after which they are solidly joined. Assuming the casing layer is overlaid, it becomes blocked by water and gases, and the mycelium passes on within the casing layer.

The most effective way to forestall overlays is to begin fruiting immediately while casing happens, yet in addition, make certain about the best circumstances to fruit from wins and begin. Ordinarily, the ideal circumstances for the overlay happen when the air is hot, extremely damp, and liable to be exceptionally warm. The initiation of the fruit body happens when the mycelium in the casing soil feels temperature and moistness contrast between the climate and the substrate.

As mycelium grows from the substrate into the casing, it eventually arrives at a breaking point where mugginess and temperature levels decrease, indicating to the mycelium that the vegetative stage is finished with and presently begins the opportunity to fruiting. Exceptionally muggy and hot circumstances forestall signifying of the edge, yet the mycelium just grows, and because it can't go elsewhere, so it grows on itself. Promptly by putting the new cased substrate under the lights, as often as possible misting, letting legitimate air, and being mindful so as not to overheat the growing region, the culture proves to be fruitful when it is prepared, and overlay doesn't occur.

Scratch and Contamination

While the casing layer is utilized, it is great to forestall touching or to work it, so you don't hurt the sensitive primordia or bring in contamination. However your best works, there is as yet when you have an overlay. Provided that this is true, you can save a casing layer by scratching it. To scratch, the casing layer, take a spotless fork and disinfect it by rubbing liquor. Then, at that point, delicately scratch the casing from down to up of the substrate layer. (Try not to contact the casing with your hands.) Make the dirt delicate however much as could reasonably be expected, while managing the profundity.

Sodden the scratched casing soil delicately and daintily and let the scratched soil incubate in the fruiting chamber as prior. On the off chance that you are to scratch more than one container, make a point to clean the fork each time after you scratch one container to keep contamination from the inconspicuous containments. The mycelium that couldn't emerge from the overlaid casings is now dead and contains a high proportion of contamination. Accordingly, the method referenced above to clean the fork each time is the best method when done as fast and sooner as conceivable after the issue is found to deal with.

Casing soil itself is impervious to contamination, and the mycelium itself is less impervious to contamination, particularly when its ages. Contamination is normally determined after a few mushrooms have been planted, and the substrate is depleted of supplements. If the contamination begins right off the bat in the casing stage, it is the indication of a containment component present in the substrate or in the casing itself. The better is to dispose of the culture in request, to begin with, the enhanced one. As saving elsewhere would be futile work since it normally spread the contamination to different containers, which can prompt further discarding.

There is one unique and extraordinary contamination that is going up against the casing soil normally. It is called Dactylium Dendroides, otherwise called spider web shape for its web-like appearance. It begins as little pinning points of straightforward white fluff on top of the casing soil layer that overgrows and covers the layer. Spider web shape is effectively spreadable between the smallest air and the containers. Hence, disposing of the contaminated cultures when it is found is better. It is permitted to replicate; it at last assaults and retains any mushrooms or primordia present in the container and minimizing them to a mush.

Sometimes, new growers commit an error to take the initial growth of mushroom mycelium into the casing soil layer for spider web shape. The genuine spider web shape grows on the uncertain layer on top of the casing soil layer from where the mushroom mycelium shows up through it from underneath. Additionally, the mushroom mycelium is dense and quickly in development.

The presence of spider web form can be tried not to sustain more than adequate and legitimate air dissemination inside the fruiting container, preventing an excess of dampness and contamination of the casing soil before the application.

Chapter 10

Growth and Therapeutic Supremacies of Psilocybin Mushrooms

Many mushroom species need a reduction in temperature or an increase in dampness to create fruit, yet P Cubensis don't. In a moist climate, with impressive gas trade and more than adequate light, the P Cubensis flourishes and fruits startlingly even before the mycelium can break out of the outer layer of the casing soil layer.

Numerous growers suggested definite misting or ventilating framework and culture be cooled by cooling it short-term in a cooler to initiate fruiting, however, we have found these methods superfluous. However long the strain is being developed, it is fruitful and has met the underlying circumstances. Accordingly, it should flourish. Thusly, the endeavors you have made to find a strong fruiting strain prior as opposed to working hard to gain fruit a frail one.

Within a couple of days of the casing, you begin to see primordia, the littlest mushrooms in their most unpredictable stage begin to shape up. Preferably, the structure inside the casing layer and not be seen as capable until they are shaped currently in a miniature or little mushroom. At the point when they arrived at this size of 1 centimeter, they begin to grow at a surprisingly quick rate and seem to arrive at standard size for the time being. When growing and getting the water from the underlying substrate and casing layer, so try to fog increasingly as expected while during misting, do take care not to water excessively.

At the point when the mushroom arrives at a legitimate size while growing, for capable spore spreading (as a rule somewhere close to 3 to 6 inches), its growth stops, and its cap enlarges, letting it show its gills to the climate. The best opportunity to yield mushrooms is not long before this point when the cover is expanded yet not broken, because, after this point, the mushrooms will never again have gained any genuine weight.

Likewise, you don't need the spores falling on the casing soil and containers, given the over-the-top number of spores manufactured by a single mushroom. Furthermore, the gases delivered in the type of germinating spores can decrease the serious fruiting process. The simplest method to advise is that when a mushroom is prepared to open, pay focus to the incomplete cover, the thin defensive layer that wraps the gills. Initially, the cap is completely joined, and the fractional shroud is covered up. As the cap begins to fan out, a shroud arises as a roundabout, light-hued band around the underside of the cap.

Collecting and Yield Cleaning

When the cap begins to straighten, the incomplete shroud grows past its ability to fan out and begins to cut away from the external edges of the gills. Finally, the fractional shroud is completely segregated from the cap, and the remaining part is joined to the strip in a skirt-like ring, called an annulus. Most preferably, you need to get your mushrooms when the halfway cloak shows up, or fresh, as the shroud begins to break. Growing mushrooms is as simple as holding them at the base and twisting and pulling them from the casing. Any piece of the mushroom that stays in the casing rots, so makes certain to eliminate everything, using forceps or a few disinfected chopsticks if important.

Do whatever it takes not to utilize hands by touching the casing layer straightforwardly, and be wary not to hurt least grown mushrooms or early stage close. At times, it is difficult to forestall disturbing or peeling close by mushrooms during yield. In that case, it is smarter to dispose of these less-evolved mushrooms is superior to leaving them behind. Disturbing them and frequently splitting them from the association with the substrate makes them quit growing and eventually brings about rotting. Try not to stress a lot over this impermanent loss, as anything energy is spent on this fruit culture is given to the following flush.

Commonly, a lot of vermiculite stalls out on the mushroom base during yielding mushrooms, leaving a divot after in the casing layer. Whenever you are finished with yielding, fill the openings with fresh, satisfactorily saturated casing soil, and return the can to the fruiting region. Following harvest during the time, there was a critical increase in the recurrence and amount to change how much water extricated from casing soil in the yielding mushrooms.

Every container should have three or up to twelve mushroom crops in a single week or between each flush. Normally, the initial not many flushes convey a plentiful number of mushrooms. Just after the fourth or fifth flush, the substrate is shrunk and diminished, and mushroom numbers are diminished to none, the substrate mass is shrunk fundamentally, and the quantity of mushrooms diminishes. Right now, the jars should be taken out, as the mycelium presence in them begins to kick the bucket. Frail or dead mycelium is bound to be contaminated with growths, which can spread to your healthy cultures.

In the long run, mushroom trunks are more agreeable and better to clean when they are fresh as opposed to dried out. Depending on the developed mushrooms, any remaining soil can be steadily incised, where the blade is situated to move downwards.

The Organic Effectiveness

From a particular measure of the substrate, what number of mushrooms should you hope to yield? The organic effectiveness of the mushroom is the inherited capacity of the mushroom to change the substrate into the mushrooms. 100 percent change implies either converting the wet mass of 25% substrate into fresh mushrooms or converting dry mushrooms through a 10% transformation of the dried substrate.

However, it is commonly prudent not to attempt to eliminate every mushroom from your containers and begin with fresh garments. Instead, typically, the quantity of fruits delivered after the third or fourth flush fundamentally diminished, and the culture is highly probably contaminated, which can immediately spread to the surrounding healthy culture.

Hallucinogenic mushrooms have been a piece of human culture since the beginning. The workmanship traces back to 5000 BC and should be visible on various continents showing how various cultures of the world have the strange healing abilities of the enchanted mushroom. Beginning in the 1960s and continuing right up until now, logical examinations are being directed to investigate the short-and long haul impacts of the dynamic ingredient of the psychoactive mushroom by which the main ingredient contains Psilocybin, and the outcomes so far have been overwhelming.

The experience of taking hallucinogenic mushrooms with the right dose intended and the setting is significant and frequently groundbreaking. Individuals taking Psilocybin have revealed feelings of prosperity, coordination, interconnected, gentle vision hallucinations, and feelings of self-regard and another definition of life. Like different hallucinogenic, intense, and some of the time terrifying encounters can be essential for the excursion of mind dreams and perception. In any case, they can be diminished to legitimate settings and care, and now and again turns into an integral piece of the groundbreaking experience.

The worth of both profound and lasting otherworldly encounters for healthy grown-ups and individuals with mental disorders can't be misjudged. A wide assortment of physical and cerebral diseases can be followed by unhealthy examples of injury, behavior, stress, and character battles. The force of magic mushrooms is an amazingly strong healing gadgets that can fix numerous illnesses in it, and science is currently showing that they can be utilized widely for remedial applications.

Savants and spiritualists have long had the point of view that a decent self is a deception. Neuroscientists presently think that they can demonstrate Psilocybin as assistance for individuals to represent this reality to the psychoactive properties of mystical mushrooms.

Specialists on the planet are exploring the force of medication change to assist people in quitting smoking. Less brutal wrongdoing; treat depression, nervousness, stress, and triggering the lasting otherworldly revelations. Also, in mentally healthy individuals, long-running profound stories are energized, particularly when joined via training in reflection and thought.

There are a few disadvantages to psilocybin studies - they are few, and depend on drug-prepared volunteers and in this manner invite the elective encounters. Yet, the examination is open, and the review can significantly affect the age at which there is a lot of tension. Psilocybin offers certain individuals a perspective, in which they push the constraints of their cognizance and hold a feeling of connectedness and ubiquity. These excursions are not transitory yet have mental impacts on progress. Even though we don't have the entire fall into the snare of mushrooms, studies give insights into how we can diminish suffering and struggle and accomplish a feeling of harmony.

Specialists have additionally indicated that Psilocybin prompts enchanted tests that can have long haul mental advantages when combined with mindfulness training. The most extreme portion of the medication, the positive mental impact for a long time, can be beneficial to the point that purchasers showed huge positive changes in intimacy, appreciation, meaning, and reason throughout everyday life, pardoning, past death, day-to-day otherworldly encounters, strict convictions, and aggressive initiatives. However, when you become oblivious, you remain in your presence without realizing your presence. You quit participating in all actuality yet remain alive. At the point when you regain cognizance, you can't recount a story. The story that unfurls in your life is only an element of your brain, not what your identity is. Be that as it may, there are different means to encounter authenticity, which you can have previously located, yet to endure. Some of the time our feelings change. Self-restrictions appear to be less severe, and we adjust to someone else or thing, as can be the case with drugs, obviously - however it can likewise happen when individuals fall head over heels. Contemplate, go out in the normal world, or know an extraordinary meeting in the minds.

Seeing the interconnectedness and continuity of presence gives a huge scope. It helps keep your issues in view. That is the reason researchers are attempting to find ways of stimulating revelation Medications can be useful, particularly since we comprehend that we presently know how the brain creates its deceptions.

Closing the Default Approach

Ordinary cognizance depends on part of the way on the brain's default mode organization (DMN). DMN is an organization of connecting regions of the brain that act as an information travel center, connecting and integrating information. As the name proposes, it is an ordinary framework for your brain.

Examining the impacts of Psilocybin on Brain-Wave-Swaying and the bloodstream, where the DNA was inactive. An elective organization of cognizance appears to create the impression that brings by using psilocybin, interconnected and profound, mystical, and extraordinary feelings. In the elective model, the brain made an alternate world that offers various feelings and feelings than regular daily existence. In this episode, the story itself was not the main person. For a brief time, an inspection of the circulation system and brain wave swaying uncovered the relationship between new, strange - yet coordinated and ordinary relationships, as though the brain were reorganizing its organization.

According to the mental hypothesis, the feeling of having an individual personality is known as the inner self. It's the limit producer, and the porter defines the boundaries and partitions me from you. The inner self is changeable, and feeling of personality, from infancy to adulthood within the relationships, and with certain practices like reflection. To live in a general public means to live within certain cutoff points to safeguard yourself as well as other people. We want the inner self to define the boundaries, to save us from the individuals who can exploit an excess of kindheartedness or open the spirit. Be that as it may, silencing the inner self can be something to be thankful for. Closing the default state changes the relationship between the cortical areas. It invigorates new ways, new feelings, and thoughts, which can lose their effect on our story, which prompts the insight that is avoided cognizant.

Experiencing this condition of obviousness can cause lasting changes even after the ending impacts of Psilocybin. For somebody who is seriously discouraged, going to brain activity with Psilocybin can remove him from any mental conviction, in which their essential structure rehashes pessimistic contemplations and feelings in a painful circle. What's more, in a mentally healthy individual, the extra viewpoint given by looking at elective cognizance can likewise work on generally speaking health. Minimal supernatural encounters with drugs have changed individuals after some time, leading to better temperaments, more pardoning, and closeness with others, more intimacy with others, and a feeling of association following a half year. Scientists accept that the memory of a medication try -

the outing - trips continue to influence individuals long after the medication is gone.

Therapists distinguish encounters of fundamental exchange as "quantum changes" in resistance to extra behavioral changes. Be that as it may, the two are not selected. The revelation addressed by Psilocybin can lead to another feeling of fervor, interest, or shock that changes behavior or new interests, dynamic travel, dance, reflection, nature, individuals, or different cultures. Also, no transient experience is pretty much as otherworldly and significant as to make each second after it is more straightforward to deal with, allowing experts to encounter the illumination, yet a battle in day-to-day existence.

A Characteristic Drug Potential for Psychotherapy and Psychiatry

This study covers the distinguishing proof of psilocybin, its authentic use in people, and the groundwork of examination that at last is indicated to its order to the Timetable I under the US Controlled Substances Act. Among other controlled substances, the worth of psilocybin has not been thought about. This conversation presents credible examinations and tests directed previously, examining the impacts of psilocybin on people and the chance of its utilization to treat the specialist disorder.

The consequences of the reference study are then contrasted with the reasoning that as of now defines psilocybin as a controlled substance drug in the US. It refers to and conducts both current and future examinations and past tests to determine the conceivable medicinal use (if any) as the aftereffects of such review.

Have you at any point felt that large numbers of the drugs recommended by experts for the treatment of specialist illnesses can be hidden by the suggestive states of patients and debilitates the specialist's capacity to defy what is going on and give fixes to the patients? In additional detail, we are discussing the capability of psilocybin and its purposes as a medicine. That can be involved pharmacological devices by proficient clinicians and specialists in the treatment of certain mental circumstances.

Across beneficial exploration, the clinical local area has become more mindful of the utilization of psilocybin. That might be available in the impacts of psilocybin. What's more, how experts can increase their understanding of the science of psilocybin, in the fields of psychiatry and brain research. Subsequently, the intricacies of the individual human brain and psilocybin affect the interpretation of the real world.

Increasing the exploration endeavors on the impacts of psilocybin on the human brain can without a doubt provide us with a more straightforward understanding of our cognizance. It tends to be a fundamental apparatus for these experts in the field of psychiatry and brain science. With the assistance of past exploration and an understanding of the impacts of these examinations on the world, modern scientists can finally begin to study and do investigate the healing capability of psilocybin according to an all-encompassing viewpoint.

Psilocybin; is usually found as a functioning substance part in various kinds of mushrooms. That had a place with psilocybe Individuals in history and indigenous gatherings have involved psilocybin for their profound growth.

Nonetheless, numerous indigenous cultures that train the utilization of psilocybin likewise have drilled their philosophical establishments that are in opposition to our modern moral understanding. Furthermore, they may not be good examples of the utilization of psilocybin in medicines. Be the ideal good example to utilize. In the Aztec faction, human penance was their custom, and they were the excited client of psilocybin. In any case, the information from the old and preliminary sources came straightforwardly from published field explores different avenues regarding aboriginal people groups that pursued severe guidelines around the utilization of these mushrooms for ceremonial purposes.

Albert Hoffman was a Swiss scientist who originally segregated psilocybin from mushrooms in 1957, and in 1958 he was likewise the principal individual to continue his examination to combine the synthetic compounds while working in Sandoz Drugs. For improving the procedures and treatment methods. Psilocybin was examined and explored by the psychotherapist and specialists in the last part of the 50s and mid-60s. By 1965 Psilocybin and different hallucinogens were lawful to utilize and have by Americans. In 1970, after inducting it into the Timetable, I controlled substances Act. It was really and formally discontinued as an examination and as a medicine component. In any case, during the 1990s, psilocybin surfaced again making it the foundation of exploration material to its consequences for human psychiatry and its belongings like hallucinations.

The outcomes delivered the results on individual discernments, visual boost, and various cases in the visual discernment that were seen by the individuals. It additionally indicated strange idea examples, tension, and sporadic sensations in the body that was tied by the climate discernments. Prior research indicated an individual's trouble in performing basic manners of thinking like fundamental mathematic estimations. At the point when it was given orally, the initial impacts became evident in the initial twenty to thirty minutes after ingestion. The peak showed up sixty to ninety-minute after ingestion, providing the insights of the client eventually. These were changing mental impacts altering discernments, cognizance, fondness, style, visual and hearable sensors, trouble in thinking, state of mind variance, and separation.

Mushrooms Preservation and Printing Spores

New mushrooms can be accumulated in the fridge for a week or so without losing their strength. They should be saved in a breathable pot, for example, a paper yet not a plastic sack, or a fixed plastic container, lined with a paper towel, with a cover somewhat mostly open. If you have any desire to save your mushrooms for quite a while, you need to protect them in some way or another, because psilocybin and its mixtures are quickly oxidized and become unmoving when presented to the climate.

The simplest and best method for storing is drying. It should be shielded from light, intensity, and dampness. Dried Psilocybin mushrooms can protect their solidarity for a long time, even years. Fresh mushrooms should be dried over a sluggish intensity of 110 degrees or low until it gets break hard. What's more, its supple impacts are at this point not accessible due to getting dry. Then, put them in a fixed container, for example, a zipper cooler sack or, notwithstanding, an intensity-free food stockpiling pack. The greatest amount of air should be removed from the pack before sealing the sack. For added security, individual packs should initially be set in auxiliary fixed sacks before freezing.

Mushrooms can likewise be crushed in a powder structure through either a flavor plant or espresso grinder in the wake of drying them out, however, they don't safeguard their power until kept put away all in all. The greatest measure of synthetic compounds is delivered into the climate.

The food dehydrator in the kitchenware is an extraordinary method for drying mushrooms, particularly with legitimate temperature control and a rotating fan. The best models flow hot air in an even course, which brings about drying them hard and fast present on all cabinet shelves. A makeshift brief food dehydrator can be immediately incorporated into a wooden box with a removable, sliding wire screen shelf and 150-watt luminous lighting bulb as its wellspring of intensity. Then again, the mushrooms can be dried out for the time being, in a hot broiler, or on the rack above the oven. Whatever dehydrating method you use, make certain to utilize light intensity, 110°F, or less. Getting dried-out mushrooms at high temperatures tastes harsh and less strong.

Printing Spores resembles tissue cloning and is one method for preserving the hereditary cosmetics of your culture. The spores are the result of sexual propagation activity, and that implies that the spore print contains many kinds of genotypes. Very much like the human propagation framework, each child is comprised of an irregular combination of characters from the core of its two parent cores.

Carefully speaking, spore printing never has the very hereditary qualities that came from mushrooms (instead of tissue cloning, which most likely does). Notwithstanding, the types of

Psilocybin mushrooms are for the most part very steady starting with one age and then onto the next, and most of the spores in print perform practically indistinguishable from their folks. Spore Printing can keep going for a long time on the off chance that they are presented to light, intensity, and dampness. In this manner, on the off chance that the clone strain is entirely lost or completely drained, these spore prints address a type of insurance.

Spore Print Making

1. To get the spore print, you require a level-covered mushroom with the gills completely open. With cloning, just the most critical and most powerful example for printing the spores, print the greatest number of spores prints conceivable.

2. Cut spotless and clear, and compliment as conceivable to give an even and consistent base. Using the tip of a blade, remove any halfway shroud marks from the gills, and prevent touching the gills straightforwardly.

3. Spore printing can be printed on paper, glass, infinitesimal slides, or aluminum foil. From these, glass or foil is the most ideal decision to make, as they can be disinfected by cleaning them with the liquor and can be dried before use, and afterward can undoubtedly be taken out their level surface from the inoculation circle. Sanitized plastic Petri dishes additionally function admirably on the off chance that the cap is adequately little to fit serenely inside them. Take different prints on a single sheet of foil, leaving a lot of room between each cap with the goal that the foil can be collapsed over to the highest point of the print for capacity. On the off chance that you are using slides, you might have to utilize numerous to cover the whole cap.

4. Let it dry after sterilizing the printing surface with liquor.

5. Put the capping face down on the printing material and wrap it with an improved container

to maintain moist air and decrease the wind stream.

6. Within the following couple of hours, the mushroom cap should have been added and printed on a sheet of paper or foil. If important, examples can be had from gradually producing tests for the time being to make thick impressions or thick print.

7. When the spore print is finished, the print should be fixed to diminish contamination. If using the foil or paper, cut out the print and crease it clean and foil it over, making sure not to squeeze it straightforwardly onto the spores underneath. Seal the edges of the paper or foil by folding them over. On the off chance that you are using a minuscule glass slide, cover the print with a disinfected clear slide and tape up the edges.

8. After folding them or taping them over, however the prints inside the zipper stockpiling sacks and imprint them with the date and

whatever other significant information that you additionally need to check.

These spore prints should be gotten in a spot far from light, dampness, and intensity, yet should not be placed in the cooler or be kept in frozen condition. Enough safeguarded spore prints keep going for a very long time.

The Physiological impacts

The physiological impacts of synthetic substances are not more apparent than the mental impacts. Additionally, the different physiological impacts of psilocybin may be influenced by the mental signs appearing that were straightforwardly connected with the mental impacts. However, research has created convincing information showing a predictable physiological reaction to synthetics in people. These physiological impacts included: enlargement of the understudies and periodic increase in circulatory strain in individuals with heart conditions like hypertension.

The most widely recognized secondary effects related to psilocybin are weakened attention to the overall setting, general feelings of uneasiness, depression, emotional changes, good and pessimistic temperaments, dizziness, ordinary degrees of focus, sickness, frenzy, and instability in maintaining examples of unusual considerations and thoughts.

Psilocybin isn't related to any illness of the human body or organ framework. Nonetheless, because of the capacity of harsh mental responses under the substance influence, a few specialists have addressed whether hallucinogens can be related to any lasting mental impacts in people. A recent report required an explicit reply to this inquiry, albeit a significant part of the emphasis had been on the drawn-out impacts that hallucinogens can have on juveniles' intellects.

Research has shown that intense maniacal disorders in youthfulness are significantly less prefer to happen with the utilization of hallucinogenic medications. Nonetheless, if psilocybin isn't utilized under the oversight of experts or individuals who don't know about the smart mental changes brought about by the synthetic, it can prompt psychosis in mentally unsound individuals. That implies that mentally tested individuals should not be administered psilocybin with its management. Otherwise, it can cause psychosis.

The hallucinogenic impacts and seriousness of nervousness or frenzy responses to psilocybin can be diminished. The members must be made mindful of the impacts of the medications all through the course. Furthermore, it should be finished before administering the medication. Specialists have additionally reasoned that, until now, there has been no immediate affirmation of the demise of psilocybin ingestion or mushrooms. That contained just psilocybin and related compounds.

Albeit the utilization of psilocybin in people involves risk factors, they have been contrasted with the utilization of different professionally prescribed tranquilizers as of now endorsed for solution in the US. For instance, psycho-energizers, for example, amphetamines are utilized to treat various circumstances, from ADD and ADHD to narcolepsy. These include feelings of uneasiness, fretfulness, crabbiness, uncertainty, nervousness, and visual deceptions. Nonetheless, a tremendous contrast between the two medications is that lawful medication containing amphetamines is bound to cause excess and passing. While illegal medications, psilocybin doesn't.

Modern exploration of psilocybin has given restricted yet dependable examinations. Such examination has prompted a more straightforward interest in the investigation into the utilization of hallucinogenics for clinical purposes. Maybe the fundamental variable for the recovery of psilocybin research is the capability of modern advancements. It assists the specialists to object, to the different social and political myths about hallucinogenic and different medications. A perfect representation of such myths can be handily found in the US government's case (Timetable I of Controlled substance) that psilocybin is almost certain to be manhandled. Ongoing investigations added to the information given by the past examinations have recommended that the potential for maltreatment of psilocybin is zero. All myths would in general be "reality" and never have a logical premise. A modern examination of psilocybin is the beginning point against the misinterpretations of its utilization. What's more, underlines the requirement for additional investigation into what these substances mean for the human body.

A long time after discontinuing the expected medicinal utilization of psilocybin. The methodology has been influenced by the US government's restriction on controlled substance misuse, particularly in the case of psilocybin.

Summary of Overall Growing Process

Stage 1: Readiness

1) Get ready jars:

With the mallet and nail, which should be disinfected by wiping with liquor, poke four holes down through every one of the covers, uniformly separated around their boundaries.

2) Get ready substrate:

For each jar, completely combine ⅔ cup vermiculite and ¼ cup water in the mixing bowl. Drain an abundance of water using the disinfected strainer.

Add ¼ cup earthy-colored rice flour per half-pint jar to the bowl, and combine with the sodden vermiculite.

3) Fill jars:

Being mindful so as not to pack too firmly, fill the jars to within a half-inch of the edges.

Sanitize this top half-inch with rubbing liquor

Top off your jars with a layer of dry vermiculite to insulate the substrate from contaminants.

4) Steam clean:

Firmly screw on the tops and cover the jars with tin foil. Secure the edges of the foil around the sides of the jars to keep water and buildup from getting through the openings.

Place the little towel (or paper towels) into the huge cooking pot and organize the jars on top, ensuring they don't contact the base.

Add regular water to a level mostly up the sides of the jars and bring it to a sluggish bubble, ensuring the jars remain upstanding.

Put the tight-fitting top on the pot and pass it on to steam for a 75-an hour and a half. If the pot dries up, replenish it with hot faucet water.

NOTE: A few growers like to utilize a strain cooker set for an hour at 15 PSI.

5) Permit to cool:

In the wake of steaming, leave the foil-shrouded jars in the pot for a few hours or short-term. They should be at room temperature before the subsequent stage.

Stage 2: INOCULATION

1) Disinfect and get ready syringe:

Utilize a lighter to warm the length of your syringe's needle until it gleams scorching. Permit it to cool and wipe it with liquor, taking into consideration not contacting it with your hands.

Pull back the unclogger a bit and shake the syringe to equally convey the psilocybin mushroom spores.

NOTE: Assuming that your syringe and needle require gathering before use, be very mindful to keep away from contamination in the process. Cleaned plastic gloves and a careful cover can help, however, the surest way is to gather the syringe inside a disinfected still-air or glove box.

2) Inject spores:

Eliminate the foil from the first of your jars and insert the syringe to the extent that it will go through one of the openings.

With the needle touching the side of the jar, inject roughly ¼ cc of the spore arrangement (or somewhat less if using a 10 cc syringe across 12 jars).

Rehash for the other three openings, wiping the needle with liquor between each utilization.

Cover the openings with micropore tape and put the jar away, leaving the foil off.

Rehash the inoculation process for the remaining jars, sterilizing your needle with the lighter and afterward liquor between every inoculation.

Stage 3: COLONIZATION

1) Hang tight for the mycelium:

Place your inoculated jars someplace wipe and far removed them. Keep away from direct daylight and temperatures outside 70-80°F (room temperature).

White, fleecy-looking mycelium should begin to show up somewhere in the range of seven and 14 days, spreading outward from the inoculation locales.

NOTE: Watch out for any indications of contamination, including unusual varieties and scents, and discard any suspect jars right away. Do this externally in a safe sack without unscrewing the tops. On the off chance that you're uncertain about whether a jar is contaminated, consistently decide in favor of alert — regardless of whether the substrate is otherwise healthily colonized — as certain contaminants are lethal.

2) Merge:

Following three to about a month, on the off chance that all works out positively, you should have something like six effectively colonized jars. Leave for an additional seven days to permit the mycelium to reinforce its hang on the substrate.

Stage 4: PREPARING THE GROW CHAMBER

1) Make a shotgun fruiting chamber:

Take your plastic stockpiling container and drill quarter-inch openings around two inches separated all around the sides, base, and cover. To abstain from cracking, drill your openings from the inside out into a block of wood.

Set the case north of four stable articles, organized at the corners to permit air to stream under. You may likewise need to cover the surface under the crate to safeguard it from dampness spillage.

NOTE: The shotgun fruiting chamber is a long way from the best plan, yet it's speedy and simple to construct and finishes the work alright for beginners. Afterward, you might need to evaluate options.

2) Add perlite:

Place your perlite into a strainer and run it under the virus tap to douse.

Permit it to drain until there are no dribbles left, then, at that point, spread it over the foundation of your grow chamber.

Rehash for a layer of perlite around 4-5 inches down.

Stage 5: FRUITING

1) "Birth" the colonized substrates (or "cakes"):

Open your jars and eliminate the dry vermiculite layer from each, taking into consideration not to harm your substrates, or "cakes," in the process.

Overturn each jar and tap down onto a disinfected surface to deliver the cakes intact.

2) Dunk the cakes:

Rinse the cakes each in turn under a virus tap to eliminate any free vermiculite, taking into consideration not to harm them.

Fill your cooking pot or one more enormous container with lukewarm water, and spot your cakes inside. Lower them just underneath the surface with another pot or correspondingly weighty thing.

Leave the pot at room temperature for as long as 24 hours, so the cakes rehydrate.

3) Roll the cakes:

Eliminate the cakes from the water and put them on a disinfected surface.

Fill your mixing bowl with dry vermiculite.

Roll your cakes individually to cover them in vermiculite completely. This will assist with keeping the dampness in.

4) Move to grow chamber:

Cut a tin foil square for every one of your cakes, huge enough for them to sit on without touching the perlite.

Space these equitably inside the grow chamber.

Put your cakes on top and delicately for the chamber with the shower bottle.

Fan with the top before closing.

5) Enhance and screen conditions:

Fog the chamber around four times each day to keep the dampness up, taking into consideration not to drench your cakes with water.

Fan with the cover up to six times each day, particularly after misting, to increase wind current.

NOTE: A few growers utilize fluorescent lighting set on a 12-hour cycle, however indirect or surrounding lighting during the day is fine. Mycelium simply needs somewhat light to determine where the outside is and where to advance mushrooms.

Stage 6: HARVESTING

1) Watch for fruits:

Your mushrooms, or fruits, will show up as tiny white knocks before sprouting into "pins." Following 5-12 days, they'll be prepared to gather.

2) Pick your fruits:

At the point when prepared, slice your mushrooms near the cake to eliminate them. Try not to sit tight for them to arrive at the finish of their growth, as they'll begin to lose power as they are a further adult.

NOTE: The best chance to reap mushrooms is just before the cover breaks. At this stage, they'll have light, cone-shaped covers and covered gills.

Psilocybin mushrooms will generally turn sour within half a month in the refrigerator. So if you intend to utilize them for microdosing or you simply need to save them for some other time, you'll have to think about capacity. The best method for long-haul stockpiling is drying. This should keep them strong for a few years for however long they're kept in a cool, dim, dry spot. On the off chance that they're put away in the cooler, they'll essentially endure indefinitely.

The lo-fi method for drying your mushrooms is to forget about them on a sheet of paper for a couple of days, maybe before a fan. The issue with this method is they will not get "saltine dry." That is, they'll in any case retain some dampness and won't snap when you attempt to twist them. Their strength may likewise essentially diminish, depending on how long you forget about them.

Using a dehydrator is by a long shot the most effective drying method, yet it very well may be costly. A decent option is to utilize a desiccant as follows:

Air dry your mushrooms for 48 hours, in a perfect world with a fan.

Place a layer of desiccant into the foundation of a sealed shut container. Promptly accessible desiccants include silica-gel kitty litter and anhydrous calcium chloride, which you can buy from a tool shop.

Place a wire rack or comparative set-up over the desiccant to hold your mushrooms back from touching it.

Orchestrate your mushrooms on the rack, ensuring they're not excessively near one another, and seal the container.

Sit tight for a couple of days, then, at that point, test to check whether they're wafer dry and snap without any problem.

Move to capacity sacks (for example vacuum-fixed Ziploc) and place them in the cooler.

REUSING THE SUBSTRATE

After your most memorable flush, similar cakes can be reused up to multiple times. Just dry them out for a couple of days and rehash Step 5.2 above (dunking). However, don't move them in the vermiculite. Simply place them back in the grow chamber and fog and fan them as in the past. At the point when you begin to see contaminants (ordinarily around the third reuse), douse the cakes with the mister shower and discard them outside in a solid pack.

Final Thoughts

If you know nothing about their belongings, your fervor and grief are at the simple commitment of bliss and shock that might be appeared in these mushrooms. We expect that you have finished your examination before you crack it on into the huge, still for the most part researchable, and consistently strange hallucinogenic impacts. Talk with individuals who have chipped away at it before you, face to face, online, or in print! The more you know, the more you comprehend it, the more you are ready for the mysteries you face, and the more fortunes you can take with you. We suggest understanding all the more obvious with the majority of the review you do. You should accept such guidance with more consideration because as usual, your review might fluctuate. Since your growing concentrate probably furnishes you with additional mushrooms than you want at some random time, you can involve them for long-haul stockpiling and sometime in the future. Psilocybin mushrooms can be eaten fresh, however, there are two elements you might need to comprehend and consider. Most importantly, fresh mushrooms are 90% water by weight, so the measurement should be increased by an element of 10 while taking fresh mushrooms. Additionally, many individuals have observed that fresh mushrooms are considerably less absorbable than shriveled ones for obscure reasons. It is seen that on fresh mushrooms utilization at least a couple of times, tormented with spasms, indigestion, and general nervousness. Drying them appears to eliminate any impacts. One method for avoiding indigestion while using fresh mushrooms is to infuse them and dispose of strong articles in the wake of steeping. If you pick freshly examined, ensure they are perfect, dependable, and freshly picked. More established, gentler fruits can have microscopic organisms and should be disposed of.

Moreover, there are somewhere around two reasons. Most importantly, as you probably are aware at this point, growing mushrooms is not a trivial issue, even with the numerous enhancements made throughout the long term. For becoming fruitful, abilities and severe discipline should be incorporated once a particular objective has been accomplished. When obtained, such abilities normally request continuous review. Second, the science and practice of fungus are so amazing and alluring that it is extremely difficult to try not to be brought into their reality, as a different province spreads quickly through a durable substrate. It is prescribed to understand an ever-increasing number of assets accessible online and in print structure. The lawful status of possessing, taking in, growing, or selling sorcery mushrooms relies upon where you reside. In the US, Psilocybin mushroom is Timetable I drug under a correction to the Controlled Substances Act, additionally called as Psychotropic Substances Act. It implies that it has a great likelihood for abuse, is as of now unsatisfactory for clinical use, and isn't protected to utilize considerably under the specialist's management. Since Psilocybin mushrooms have psilocybin, which is a Psychotropic substance in wizardry mushrooms, it is for the most part explained that mushrooms are unlawful in themselves. Nonetheless, because mushroom spores don't contain psilocybin, some have pointed it to be uncertainty in government regulation. Magic mushrooms are for the most part liable to state regulation (except if they are in huge amounts), and most states have a prohibition on their ownership. As of late, in any case, urban communities and states have started to rethink their standpoint on psilocybin mushrooms. Denver turned into the principal city 2019, in the US to make sorcery mushrooms decriminalized. States like St Nick Cruz and Auckland and California followed the suit. Despite these accomplishments, mushroom legitimization exercises are working hard in different states. In Oregon, California, and Iowa, officials have introduced bills repealing mushroom decriminalization. In any part of the world, it is legitimate to possess and sell fresh mushrooms and spores (dried mushrooms are quite often unlawful). However, the laws of such controlled substances are different among different nations. For instance, until 2005, selling fresh wizardry mushrooms was legitimate in the UK. The ownership of spores is as yet legitimate. The Netherlands, somewhere else known as an unlawful medication center point, prohibited the offer of dried mushrooms in 2001 and fresh mushrooms in 2008, yet you need some "magic truffles." Such are the mushrooms that are not completely ready hence deviating from the law. Mexico has a total prohibition on mushrooms except if otherwise they are utilized for strict purposes. In Spain, mushrooms are decriminalized, however, growing units may not function admirably with specialists. In different nations, it would be lawful to keep them but not sell them. What's more, in others, punishments can be extreme. In Indonesia, for instance, specialists some of the time give capital punishment to such individual substances. In other different areas of the planet, there is no interest in making strategies or punishing mushroom growers or buyers. Mushrooms are a legitimate element in Jamaica, the Bahamas, and Brazil. A few nations, like Mexico, have prohibited the utilization of magic mushrooms by the neighborhood populace's strict services.

GLOSSARY

Agar A polysaccharide (a sugar-like particle) found in the cell walls of certain green growth. At the point when disintegrated in boiling water and afterward cooled, it to some degree cement, similar to gelatin. Used to make semi-strong media for culturing growths and different microorganisms.

Agonist A substance that initiates a physiological reaction when bound to a receptor.

Alkaloid Any of a class of nitrogen-containing alkaline natural compounds of normal origin; a significant number of them have articulated physiological consequences for people. Psilocybin, morphine, strychnine, and caffeine are all alkaloids.

Allelochemical A compound delivered by a living creature that has a impact upon different creatures in its current circumstance.

Amine A nitrogen-containing, fundamental natural particle,

Annulus The tissue leftovers of the halfway cover that remain appended to the stipe as a membranous ring.

Aseptic strategy The avoidance of living microorganisms from media, what's more, the workplace however the utilization of sterilization and air filtration.

Autoclave To disinfect using the utilization of high tensions and temperatures.

Autotroph An organic entity that can shape nourishing natural substances from basic inorganic substances like carbon dioxide.

Baeocystin

4-phosphoryloxy-N-methyltryptamineT is an indole alkaloid delivered by numerous types of Basidiomycete growths.

Basidiomycetes A class of higher parasites distinguished by having their spores borne on a basidium.

Basidium The minute club-shaped structure whereupon are borne the spores of certain parasites.

Binomial The novel two-section Latin name given to a type of creature, consisting of the class followed by the particular designation (e.g., Psilocybe cubensis).

Natural proficiency The inherent capacity of a mushroom animal types to convert the materials of its substrate into mushrooms. 100 percent B..E. implies a 25% chance of the wet substrate weight into fresh mushrooms, or 10% of the dry substrate into dried. bioluminescence The biochemical creation of light by living beings.

Message to the Reader

Written by a genius author this guide brings the Psilocybin mushroom growing procedures to your fingertips. After years of research, the experienced author points out the necessary guidelines which should be followed while growing the magic mushrooms and gives an interactive and caring manual to assist you with processing and culturing. Every section begins with an outline and gives important information that everyone should know about the propagation of mushrooms. The author insightfully guides you to consider the equipment used, period, and storage of the mushrooms after growth. The author has indeed composed a smart guide for magic mushrooms and it is considerably more than a book about culturing mushrooms; it is a great guide to help people that fail to culture mushrooms as per their choice. The book is written for all those who are unaware of the magical effects of magical mushrooms. A ton of endeavors have been placed into compiling the book. Do look at additional books and give your positive opinions. We will see the value in the evaluation from you!